MS
CHUTZPAH EXPRESS
MEATLOAF
FRESH MOZZARELLA
VEGGIE BURGER
FENNEL PUREE
SH

ONIONS
STARD
PICO DE LETTUCE
FRIED SHALLOT
HEESE
CANADIAN BACON
IT MUST HAVE BE
YOU WERE KISS
MPATHY FOR THE DEVIL
HICKEN
BEEF
NO. 7 SUB CLUB
RED ONION
SHRIMP MUCHIM
FRIED CLAMS
MATOES
FRIED EGG
GRAPE JELL MAYO
AYO
TOMATO MUCHIM
VEGGIE BURGER
BACON
GRANNY SMITH APPLE
THIS WILL BE OUR YEAR
.7 STEAK SAUCE
GOLD HAT
MAYO
BACON VON BRAUNHUT
CURRY CHICKEN SALAD
ICEBERG LETTUCE
EET POTATOES
BROCCOLI FALAFEL
FRIED SQUID
AVOCADO
LED PEÑOS
HAM
ROASTED CAULIFLOWER
LIME SEGMENT
FENNEL PUREE
SMOKED FRENCH DRESSING
FATHER II
MUCHIM PICKLES
RAISIN RELISH
SANDWICHES FALL APART
THE #2 BEST NEW SANDWICH IN AMERICA IN 2012 ACCORDING TO THE HUFFINGTON POST
POTATO CHIPS
YO
TOMATOES
MUSSELS
CRISPED PEPPERON
TAKEN 2
MOZZARELLA
OLD BAY CURRY SAUCE
PICKLED MUSHROOMS
ERAL IGNACIO'S CHICKEN
JCVD
VEFORT
CILANTRO
BRUSSELS SPROUTS
GRANNY SMITH APPLE
RED ONIONS
THE BATTLE OF PUEBLA
LECHE DE TIGRE MAYO
YELLOW SQUASH SAUCE
SCALLIONS
JICAMA SALAD
HUMMUS
CEVICHE
POSITIVE MENTAL ATTITUDE
ROAST BEEF
PICKLED RED ONIONS
MI CORAZÓN LLORA
ED ONIONS
DON'T CRY FOR ME ARGENTINA
SCRAMBLED EGGS
D SHALLOTS
SMOKED FRENCH DRESSING
FRIED BROCCOLI
SMOKED GOUDA CHEESE
OPERATION CORNERSTONE
CHORIZO
KETCHUP
LAZARD'S REVENGE
SCRAMBLED EGGS
SWISS CHEESE
BROCCOLI EGG & CHEES
GRILLED BOLOGNA
RUSSIAN DRESSING
PICKLED JALAPEÑOS
GARAM MASALA CORNED BEEF
THAT TIME CHRIS PARNELL PLAYED BENEDICT ARNOLD ON DRU HISTORY, THE SANDWICH
ARUGULA
GRAPE & CELERY SALAD
THE EMPIRE STRIKES BACK
SPECIAL SAUCE
THIS IS A CHICKEN SANDWICH
POACHED EGG MUCHIM

A SUPER UPSETTING COOKBOOK ABOUT SANDWICHES

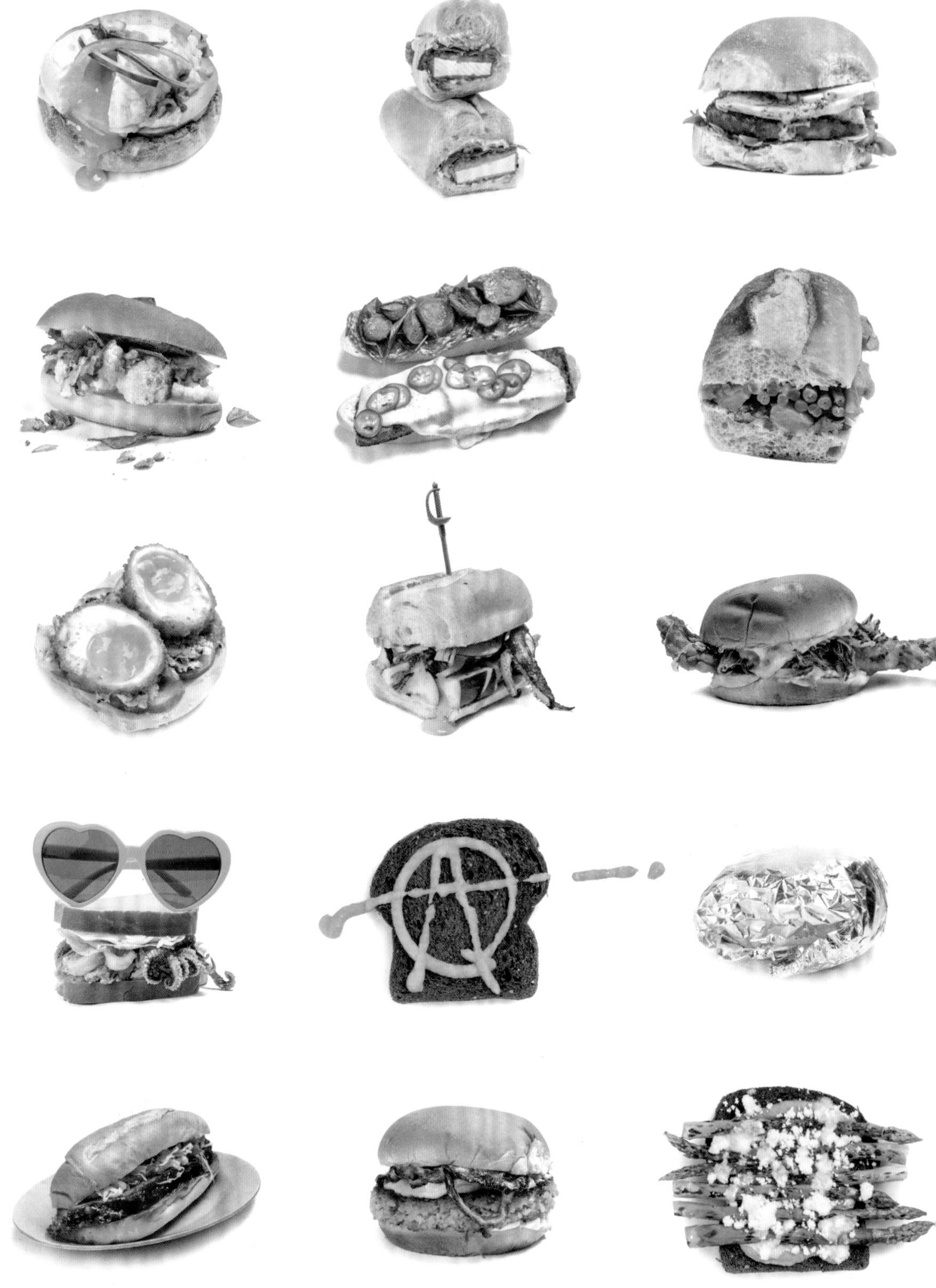

A SUPER UPSETTING COOKBOOK ABOUT SANDWICHES

• TYLER KORD •

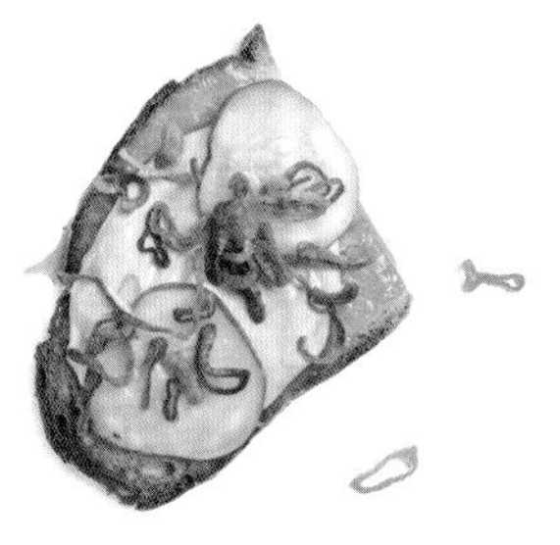

COLLAGES BY
William Wegman

PHOTOGRAPHS BY
Noah Fecks

CLARKSON POTTER/PUBLISHERS
NEW YORK

CONTENTS

Foreword

When Tyler and I were first married, he didn't cook at all. It was the summer of 1956, and we were living in a rural village in southern France, a far cry from the Lower East Side orphanage where we'd grown up. It was the army that brought us to France, though Tyler's work was classified (codes, bombs, that kind of thing) and so we couldn't discuss what he did during the hours he spent on the base. Still, it was a largely happy time, the two of us and our adopted chickens and goats roaming around the mountainous village, none of us fluent in French.[1]

There was one grocer nearby, but I soon discovered that he saved all of his good produce for the local women, and when I arrived, he would only have one vegetable to sell me: broccoli. Every evening, I tried to rally when Tyler came home on his motorbike, his face dusty with French dirt from the bumpy road through the mountains, but at last, after several weeks of pretending that I had, in fact, chosen to purchase only a single vegetable, I gave in, and told him how we'd been shamed.[2] He held me, and we wept, missing our orphan friends back home.

Still, we made do. We plucked our chickens and boiled them. We fried eggs. We baked loaves of bread, and when we were feeling indulgent, bought pastries in the village. And we stared at the mounds of broccoli on our small countertop. Back home, in America, fresh vegetables had been a rarity. Our regular diet had consisted of pickles and potatoes, with a sprig of dill in our soup. We didn't know what to do—and I, a girl of 18,[3] felt like a failure as a housewife.[4]

One morning, I came into the kitchen to discover Tyler already there. I asked him what he was doing, but he was so deep into whatever it was that he couldn't hear me speaking. I stepped closer, peered over his shoulder, and discovered seventeen plates of broccoli: fried broccoli, roasted broccoli, broccoli smothered with a mysterious brown sauce he claimed was Chinese, broccoli with cheese he'd made from our goats' milk. More and more broccoli, everywhere I looked.

"My love," I said to him.

Tyler turned to look at me, my voice having finally reached him. "Try the sandwich," he said, and handed me a plate.

If it hadn't been for the army, we would have returned to America that day. The future was so clear—Tyler and I would open a string of sandwich shops, all of them devoted to broccoli. The sandwich in my hand was so simple—roasted broccoli, cheese and nuts that must have cost him a week's stipend, plus some shallots he had fried on the stove—but it tasted like heaven.[5] I began to cry. I knew that he was too responsible to abandon his top-secret military post (those codes/bombs weren't going to break themselves), but I also knew that no one else could do what he had done. And so we stayed in France, knowing that another life was possible.

By the time our sixth child[6] was born, all of them native French speakers, the local grocer softened, and began to offer us other ingredients, which Tyler would then add into his repertoire, often cooking all night, after the children and I had gone to bed.[7] His sandwiches were works of art, containing his heart and soul. When the zeppelin accident killed my darling Tyler at the age of 73, I thought his sandwiches had died with him. Luckily, two of our grandchildren, Henri and Emile Kord, charming young Frenchmen, have compiled their beloved Papa's recipes in this volume, along with many of his own words, scribbled in secret during his army years. Their English is not perfect, but neither was his.

Rest in peace, my love, knowing that your broccoli will live forever.

—*Emma Straub*[8]

---

1 We're not married. In fact, by publication time, we will both be married to other people. Not only are we not married, and married to other people, but in fact we never even dated. But just go with it.

Also, we aren't really orphans. In fact, when I used to work at a bookstore in Brooklyn, Tyler's mother would often come in and chat with me. She is a lovely woman. My parents are okay too. Tyler's father is probably lovely also but I never met him, so I can't say for sure.

2 This would probably happen to me.

3 I didn't actually get married until I was 28, don't worry.

4 But I'm still a failure at being a housewife.

5 This is really how I feel about Tyler's sandwiches.

6 Six is a lot, but why not go for it, you know?

7 Once, when we were in college, I stayed up late doing karaoke with Tyler and his friends, and one of them sang Queen's "Fat-Bottomed Girls," which I took as a compliment, whether or not it was intended as such.

8 *New York Times* bestselling author of *The Vacationers, Laura Lamont's Life in Pictures,* and *Other People We Married*; Oberlin class of 2002, sandwich lover, married to someone other than Tyler

Introduction

What's better than sandwiches?!?! Falling in love, action movies, nephews, Led Zeppelin, becoming super good friends with Tom Cruise to name a few. But sandwiches are really great too! I eat a lot of sandwiches, I make a lot of sandwiches, and I think about sandwiches a lot. But is there really anything to say about sandwiches that hasn't already been said? And do you really want to spend ~~$35~~ ~~$30~~ ~~$25~~ $22.99 on a book about them? *

Maybe! Because this book is about more than sandwiches. I'm not the best chef in the world. But I am a notable chef in one of the most important restaurant cities in the world, and I have a bunch of restaurants and sandwich shops that some people who are not related to me love. And when I cook for people, I want to make things that nobody would think to make at home because it sounds so crazy. At my restaurants, I will never offer you a BLT because you can either do that at home or go to a restaurant where they don't care about being awesome. I will never make you a ham and Swiss sandwich. Unless of course that's what you really want, and then I'll make it for you.

But I would much *rather* make you roasted cauliflower and smoked French dressing, or meatloaf with pickled shrimp, or fried zucchini with onion puree. Look, I got extremely sick once on the way to work, and you know what I did? I went to the bathroom and cried, and proceeded to work for ten hours through incredible pain, not because I wanted to make money, but because I wanted to make people *emotionally* sick because of how exciting the food was! Does that make sense? It does to me, but as time goes on I keep hearing that there are a lot of things that make sense to me that don't make a ton of sense to everybody else. I drink a lot. That is an example and a possible cause.

I am of a mind that anything can make a good sandwich as long as it is good food. And after reading this book, I hope you'll think about food in a way that is less about traditions or cultures, and more about flavors and textures, how they go together and how you can make food that is insane(-ly good) if you let go of how things are supposed to be. I have let go of how things are supposed to be in most areas of my personal life, and maybe you'll think about that too. Also, all of the components of these sandwiches can be used to make food on plates. When you're having company, sometimes it's nicer to put food on plates because "a dinner party of sandwiches" sounds like a cry for help.

So maybe there is more to say about making awesome sandwiches. It's not rocket science, but neither was my first kiss, *First Blood*, my sister Emily's first childbirth, "Communication Breakdown," or all of the thousands of letters I've written to Jerry Maguire. So let's have our own little dinner party of sandwiches!

* If you got this book as a gift, happy birthday, and I wouldn't let it get to me that your friends think you don't know how to make a sandwich. I mean, I do it professionally, and sometimes it's really hard putting things on bread. I wouldn't dwell on it.

Notes on How to Use this "Cookbook"

Every time I talk about salt, I am talking about Diamond Crystal Kosher Salt. It's not that it tastes better or has a nicer texture, it's just what I'm used to. But all salt is different, and if you use Morton's and follow these recipes as written, you will be super bummed because your food will be too salty. Of course, if you don't feel like buying a different kind of salt just for this stupid book, simply season to taste and maybe don't count on the salt measurements to be accurate.

•

I put maple syrup in almost everything I eat. It's not in so many of the recipes in this book, but I wanted to tell you about it anyway. The maple syrup I use comes from Deep Mountain Maple in West Glover, Vermont, and I recommend that you get some because it is awesome. But any legitimate maple syrup will work. Do not use the maple-flavored corn-syrup grocery-store stuff. It is delicious, I am not denying that, but the artificial flavor is a little overpowering.

•

My editor, Francis Lam, is a patient and beautiful man. He deleted so many horrible things, but he couldn't just delete the entire book or he and I would both get in trouble. What is left is the best that I am capable of, and if you don't like it, I will have to move in with Francis. He doesn't deserve that.

•

Actually, I'm a pretty great roommate. I am not home much and I'm pretty tidy. If this book is poorly received and you are looking for a roommate, please e-mail dreams@no7sub.com.

•

I don't think there are any two ingredients that can't go together. Just because they come from opposite ends of the world does not mean that they will magically taste gross when combined. Nature did not try to find a way to make sure you wouldn't put cheese on Chinese broccoli. People did that. Remember Pangaea!!

•

I didn't write an equipment section for the book. I told Francis I would, but then I didn't. The thing is, there isn't anything weird, equipment-wise, to make these recipes, maybe except for a smoker you'll use once; if you don't have a smoker (and why would you have that?), then you can go on the Internet and learn how to make or buy one. It's not that I'm too amazing to waste my time explaining it, but I'll probably be really confusing because I'll fill the explanation with all kinds of nonsense about my personal life, and that could be dangerous. I am divorced and have two different women's names tattooed on my body. And if you find a website that will give you clear and safe advice about smokers, then we're probably all better off in the long run.

•

Look at the photos and read the recipes all of the way through before you start them. I learned that in culinary school. But also, I won't be mad if your food doesn't look like mine, and neither should you. I used to think that cooking from books was lame, but I recently cooked a recipe that my girlfriend's mother gave me. Because I was following somebody else's instructions to the letter, the most miraculous thing happened: my apartment smelled *like somebody else was cooking*. Being able to follow a recipe is like being able to read music, and you should feel free to make it your own a little, because nobody will mind if you like your broccoli a little more cooked than I do. And if the recipe doesn't make any sense, then it's probably because I am crazy and sometimes ignored the notes of the recipe testers because I like things to get a little weird.

ROAST BEEF

Altered Beef

*Hot Roast Beef, Jus, Fresh Mozzarella,
Roasted Onions, Pickled Bean Sprouts*

•

Chutzpah Express

*Roast Beef, Pickled Mushrooms,
Chinese Mustard, Parsley*

•

Don't Cry for Me Argentina

*Roast Beef, Roasted Onions, Pickled Red Onions,
Fried Shallots, Smoked French Dressing, Scallions*

•

This Will Be Our Year

*Roast Beef, Fried Clams, Tomato Muchim,
Grape Jelly Mayo*

I know every chef on TV says that if you don't get a nice sear on your roast beef you won't "lock in the juices" and it will make children cry, but they are lying to you because they are insecure and don't make decisions for themselves. You can make your own decisions, so try something different. Do you caramelize the cucumbers for your cucumber salad? No? Why not? It will seal in the juices and taste better. How stupid does that sound, right?

So anyway, I'm calling this roast beef, but it's more of a slow-cooked beef than a super-caramelized tough-guy thing. With a slow cook you can get a nice even temperature throughout, without an overcooked gray ring, and we coat the beef in a delicious dark rub so that people won't make a big deal out of the non-brown color. Also, this technique will give you a beautiful, perfectly cooked chunk of beef without splattering grease all over your kitchen and setting off the smoke alarm. And the flavor will be different but just as amazing.

Now, your choice of beef does matter. If, for some reason, you have a deli slicer, you can rock out on one of the tasty, tough muscles (eye round, top round, etc.) and slice it super thin, but if you don't and you'll be slicing your beef by hand, you'll probably want to go with something more tender from the back (sirloin, tenderloin, etc.). Talk to your butcher about it. The more-tender cuts are great if you don't want to take a bite of the sandwich and pull all of the roast beef out with it.

ROAST BEEF

Makes a huge roast beef that will be enough for 8 to 12 sandwiches, or you can pick at it and slowly eat it over the course of a week

1 chunk of beef, 2 to 3 pounds

Kosher salt

2 tablespoons (¼ stick) unsalted butter

2 tablespoons Fried Shallots (PAGE 175)

2 tablespoons ancho chile powder

2 tablespoons kecap manis (sweet soy sauce) or molasses with a pinch of salt

1 tablespoon white vinegar

Preheat the oven to 250°F.

Season the beef generously, all over, with salt.

Melt the butter and combine with the shallots, chile powder, kecap manis, and white vinegar. Rub it all over the beef like you want to spend the rest of your life with that beef and no other beef (but don't make any promises to that beef or it will wind up hating you for the rest of its life). At this point it would be best to put that beef in a container and let it hang in the refrigerator overnight. But you're impulsive and want to eat beef now. Okay, well then cook it, don't be afraid; your parents always knew you were impulsive. That's why, despite a lot of questioning and private conversations, they finally accepted your choice to be a cook instead of a college professor. Time heals all wounds, but roast beef waits for no man. Cook like you were born to do.

Put the beef in a roasting pan and cook it forever. Or 2 to 2½ hours. I like my beef rare, but you decide. I vote medium, tops. Medium is as tender as beef gets before it starts to dry out and get tough again. You may use a thermometer if you'd like, and it should read 120°F for rare, 140°F for medium.

Let your cooked beef hang out on the counter for 30 minutes to rest and then put it in the refrigerator to cool completely. Cold meat is much easier to slice thin than warm or hot meat.

Hot Roast Beef • Jus • Fresh Mozzarella • Roasted Onions • Pickled Bean Sprouts

ALTERED BEEF

Makes 4 sandwiches

I spend a fair amount of time thinking about sandwiches and New York City. That's not weird because I own some sandwich shops in New York City. That said, if my sandwich shops don't exist in New York City when you read this, know that I did everything in my power to keep selling sandwiches in New York City for less than they were worth. I basically ran a sandwich nonprofit that employed people and provided discounted sandwiches, considering that I paid my staff well and used nice ingredients. If my sandwich shops do still exist, then nice work everyone!

Anyway, when I think of sandwiches in New York City, I first think of egg and cheese on a roll from a bodega. That's the unofficial official sandwich of this town. But our city has history with hot roast beef sandwiches (maybe not as much as Boston, but seriously, the best thing Boston ever did was that tea party thing, and who even remembers that now?). The hot roast beef at Brennan and Carr in Sheepshead Bay is ridiculous. The one at Roll-n-Roaster, coincidentally also in Sheepshead Bay, is even better in my opinion. But the best hot roast beef sandwich in New York—and this is totally just my stupid opinion—is at Defonte's in Red Hook. They take a chunk of roast beef out of a steam table, slice it, spoon on some jus, and top it with a thin sliver of cold fried eggplant and some fresh mozzarella cheese. I want one now so bad. This is my ode to that most perfect of beef sandwiches.

(RECIPE CONTINUES)

2 pounds meaty bones*

2 broccoli stems, cut into ½-inch disks

1 medium onion, halved

1 2-inch piece of ginger, cut into chunks and smashed

2 garlic cloves, smashed

2 tablespoons vegetable oil (optional)

1 tablespoon yellow miso paste

2 teaspoons kosher salt

2 cups Roasted Onions (PAGE 172)

1 pound Roast Beef (PAGE 13), sliced thin

4 kaiser rolls, cut open

1 6-ounce (or so) ball of fresh mozzarella, cut into 8 slices

1 cup drained Pickled Bean Sprouts (PAGE 181)

Fresh dill to taste

Fresh cilantro to taste

Preheat the oven to 375°F.

In a large roasting pan, combine the bones, broccoli stems, onion, ginger, and garlic. If your bones don't have any fat, add 2 tablespoons of vegetable oil and toss everything with it. Put the pan in the oven and roast until everything is well caramelized, about 40 minutes.

Scoop everything into a large stockpot but pour off the fat. With the roasting pan set over low heat, add a little water and scrape up all the browned bits on the bottom. Add this water to the stockpot.

Add the miso, salt, and 4 quarts of water to the pot, bring to a boil over high heat, reduce the heat, and simmer for 2 hours. If the water level gets too low, add a little more, but you want to end up with about a quart of liquid. After 2 hours, strain the stock, rinse the pot, and put the stock back into the pot.

Add the roasted onions and sliced beef, turn the heat to high, and bring back to a simmer to heat the beef through. Turn off the heat.

Lay the kaiser rolls out, cut sides up, and, using tongs, divide the beef and onions between the 4 bottom rolls. If you are really into this, add a spoonful of the broth on top. This is going to be messy, but we are comfortable with that. Top each sandwich with 2 slices of mozzarella, some pickled bean sprouts, dill, and cilantro. Reserve the broth for something awesome. Maybe some ramen noodles, or you could cook some beans with it. This sandwich will make you feel like Superman.

---

* I like duck bones for this, but the bones of pretty much any land-dwelling animal will work great, as long as there's some meat scraps left on them.

Roast Beef • Pickled Mushrooms • Chinese Mustard • Parsley

CHUTZPAH EXPRESS

Makes 4 sandwiches

This sandwich is what roast beef dreams are made of. Beef with mustard is a diet rich in sodium and relatively low in fat that Jews like me have used to sustain ourselves on this planet for so long. Eating beef with mustard is how [redacted] good.

- 2 pounds Roast Beef (PAGE 13), sliced thin
- 4 kaiser rolls, split in half
- Chinese mustard to taste
- 1 cup Pickled Mushrooms (PAGE 174), drained
- ½ cup fresh parsley leaves

Put ½ pound of roast beef on each split roll. Top with the mustard, mushrooms, and parsley. Serve this one for brunch. You know how some people get together for brunch? Sometimes the very idea of having people over for brunch makes me question life to a degree. I mean, they come over, you eat, they don't leave for a while, they want to drink during the day (which always ruins everything!), and then suddenly it's dinnertime, and I'm left trying to figure out what the point of everything is. Because aren't you *supposed* to spend time with your friends, eating and drinking and enjoying each other's company? Because I don't really like doing that. Does that mean that work is the only thing that matters? LOL.

Roast Beef • Roasted Onions • Pickled Red Onions • Fried Shallots • Smoked French Dressing • Scallions

DON'T CRY FOR ME ARGENTINA

Makes 4 large sandwiches that will make you forget about the 2014 World Cup

I love onions so, so much. Yes, they make me cry, but a lot of things make me cry. This sandwich is a celebration of the onion! If you are vegetarian but you still want to celebrate onions, you could swap out the roast beef for cauliflower, broccoli, seitan, or whatever you have. Or you could make a giant papier-mâché onion, but the sandwich is probably easier.

- **4 Italian sub loaves, cut in half lengthwise**
- **1 cup Roasted Onions (PAGE 172)**
- **2 pounds Roast Beef (PAGE 13), sliced thin**
- **½ cup Smoked French Dressing (PAGE 162)**
- **1 cup Pickled Red Onions (PAGE 173)**
- **¼ cup Fried Shallots (PAGE 175)**
- **2 scallions, sliced thin**

Preheat the oven to 375°F.

Put all of the bread pieces on a baking sheet, cut side up. Put some of the roasted onions on each half. Put them in the oven and cook until the onions are warm and the bread is toasted, about 6 minutes.

Put ½ pound of roast beef on each of the 4 bottom pieces of bread. Drizzle some smoked French dressing on each sandwich. Top each sandwich with a quarter of the pickled red onions, fried shallots, and scallions. Put the tops on the sandwiches and serve.

Roast Beef • Fried Clams • Tomato Muchim • Grape Jelly Mayo

THIS WILL BE OUR YEAR

Makes 4 sandwiches about the size of an enormous hot dog

Fuck a lobster roll. I'm sorry, Luke's Lobster, you guys make the best lobster rolls in New York City, but you New England motherfuckers have been coming to New York for years, putting lobster in a hot dog bun and making us all argue about it to distract us from realizing that you are cleaning up and sending all of the money back to Maine. Seriously, we're all bickering about how a lobster roll should have butter but not mayo, but mayo but not butter, but celery, but pickles—but what are we even talking about? Lobster always tastes good on a hot dog bun, end of discussion!

I would like to propose this sandwich as New York's answer to a lobster roll. And then we will sell it in Boston and Providence and a city in Maine (if I could actually name one), and you guys can argue over what is a "real" New York beef and clam roll! And screw you!

I borrowed a hot dog bun from Luke's Lobster for this photo, so also, thank you, and I love you! Especially Scott! I am not healthy in any way.

- 1 tablespoon unsalted butter
- 4 split-top hot dog buns
- ½ cup Grape Jelly Mayo, a.k.a. Genius Russian Dressing (PAGE 160)
- 1 pound Roast Beef (PAGE 13), sliced thin
- 4 slices Tomato Muchim (PAGE 69), cut into half-moons
- 1 recipe Fried Clams (PAGE 146)

Melt the butter over medium-low heat in a sauté pan large enough to hold all 4 hot dog buns. Dip both sides of each bun in the butter and then let them ride on one side until golden brown. Flip them and get them golden on the other side, about 5 minutes per side.

Open the buns and put a little grape jelly mayo in each one. Stuff in some roast beef, a couple of tomato slices, and the clams. Eat while drinking beers, saving the bottles, and driving to Maine, where you will throw all of the bottles at lobster fishermen [This seems like a terrible way to introduce yourself. —Ed.], open a beef-and-clam-roll truck, and make a better life for yourself than you have in this terrible soul-crushing city.

CHICKEN

The Frito Kid

Roasted Chicken, Black Bean Hummus,
Fritos, Lettuce, Tomato

•

No. 7 Sub Club

Roasted Chicken, Canadian Bacon, Pico de Lettuce,
Tomatoes, Jalapeño Mayo, BBQ Chips

•

This Is a Chicken Sandwich

Roasted Chicken, Fried Eggplant,
Fresh Mozzarella, Arugula, Special Sauce

•

Sandwiches Fall Apart

Curry Chicken Salad, Avocado, Iceberg Lettuce,
Fried Squid, Lime Segments

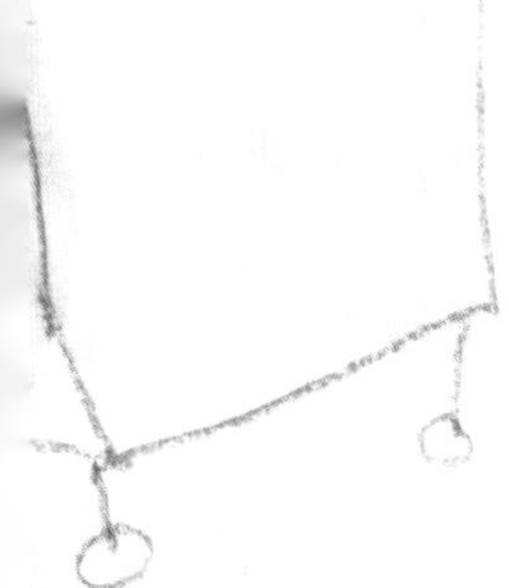

ROASTED CHICKEN

Makes so much chicken or makes 1 chicken

I'm generally not a fan of cooking an entire animal in one piece. Animals' legs work harder, so they're tougher and need to cook longer to become tender, whereas the chest of a flightless bird—or the back of a mammal that never lifts anything—is soft and doesn't require too much cooking. If you cooked a cow whole, you would have to make a choice: either you cook it until the legs are tender but the loin and tenderloin are dry and disgusting, or you cook the back meat perfectly and the legs are too tough to eat. A chicken is a much less dramatic version of that. I like the legs hammered and the breast just-cooked. It is possible to very nearly nail it with a whole bird, but that window is tight and not all of us are that in tune with our poultry.

That said, we're going to shred this bird and put it on a stupid sandwich, so let's accept whole-bird cookery. But if you really want to show everybody who is boss, separate the legs from the breasts and roast them separately. Or you could just roast the legs and save the breasts to make the most maligned dish in the history of food: Boneless, Skinless Chicken Breasts. But we'll get to that in a minute.

1 chicken, about 3 pounds
Kosher salt to taste
Canola oil

Preheat the oven to 400°F.

Season the chicken thoroughly with salt and rub with oil. Put it in a roasting pan, breast side up, and into the oven. It should take about an hour to cook. If you've cut it into pieces, cook them skin side up; the breasts should take about 30 minutes, and the legs should take 45. My oven sucks, so I throw it under the broiler for the last 5 minutes to brown the skin.

If you'd like a more detailed recipe for roasted chicken, maybe read a better book than this one. My 1968 edition of *Mastering the Art of French Cooking* by Julia Child has some words of wisdom on pages 240 to 241.

When the chicken is cooked, pull it out and let it cool. Shred that beast into a bowl. Save the bones to make chicken noodle soup.

BONELESS, SKINLESS CHICKEN BREASTS

Makes enough chicken breast for 4 sandwiches, unless you are paleo, and then it makes one triumphant meal

Boneless, skinless chicken breasts have become the epitome of flavorless food. This is because chefs on TV are unimaginative and lack finesse. Yes, an under-seasoned, overcooked chicken breast is a bummer. So is an under-seasoned, overcooked rib eye. But a perfectly seasoned, perfectly cooked chicken breast is one of the absolute greatest things that anybody ever put on a sandwich. It does take a little skill though, so I understand why a lot of chefs hate it. Hate comes from fear, and nothing is more frightening for a chef than to overcook something seen by the world as easy to prepare. And how weird is it when chefs profess to hate certain foods anyway? You don't hear musicians complaining about certain notes, do you?

We're going to cook chicken in boiling water, which doesn't sound exciting. But it's quick and easy when you don't want to spend an hour roasting chicken.

1 garlic clove, smashed

¼ yellow onion, sliced thin

½ teaspoon fresh thyme leaves or ¼ teaspoon dried thyme

1 tablespoon olive oil

1½ teaspoons kosher salt

2 boneless, skinless chicken breasts (8 to 12 ounces total)

In a medium saucepan, combine the garlic, onion, thyme, olive oil, salt, and ¾ cup of cold water. Lay the chicken breasts on top.

Bring the water to a boil over high heat, flipping the chicken occasionally, until all of the water is evaporated and the chicken begins to sizzle in the oil a little, 8 to 10 minutes. The chicken should be firm to the touch, and if you pull back the tenderloin, it should be just a tiny bit pink. Transfer the chicken to a plate and spread the cooked onions on top of it because they are delicious. Let it rest for an additional 5 minutes; it will finish cooking during this time. Keep whole, slice, or shred.

WARNING: This chicken has not reached an internal temperature of 165°F, which is required for killing salmonella. It is undercooked according to the United States government. So if you are worried that your chicken is carrying the salmonella virus, then maybe you want to add more water and keep cooking it.

I do not take salmonella lightly, but that's why I'm super anal about cleaning, avoiding cross-contamination, and buying nice poultry. I've never had salmonella and don't plan on it. I'm not telling you that if you follow this recipe you will definitely not get salmonella, but I am saying that if you cook your chicken to 165°F, you will find out why many chefs think that boneless, skinless chicken breasts are not good.

Roasted Chicken • Black Bean Hummus • Fritos • Lettuce • Tomato

THE FRITO KID

Makes 4 subs that are too big to eat right before bedtime

There's a Subway ad on TV right now for the new "Fritos Chicken Enchilada," which is a sandwich featuring chicken and Fritos. I have no idea if they're trying to copy me or not. I mean, I didn't invent the idea of putting chips on a sandwich, even though I do it all the time and everyone knows it's kind of my thing and I work in New York, where we have real subways. So maybe this sandwich is an unintentional ode to Subway. But you should use food instead of whatever it is that they put in their sandwiches. I'm not sure what kind of meat anybody expects to get for so little money, but it seems pretty clear that it won't come from a happy and healthy animal. I, for one, would be more comfortable with the idea that a Taco Bell taco is made of a tiny bit of beef, some beef fat, soybeans, sawdust, and Styrofoam than thinking that they are raising cows in the conditions required to fill a taco with 2 ounces of actual beef for the same price as a bottle of water. Sometimes water actually costs more! And it literally falls *from the sky*!!! People want their beef to cost less than that? And then they're mad that it tastes like it's made by mixing equal parts of beef and used yoga mats?! Anyway, this chapter is about chicken, but you get the idea.

3 cups shredded Roasted Chicken (PAGE 26) or 3 Boneless, Skinless Chicken Breasts (PAGE 27)

1 tablespoon olive oil or the drippings from the roasting pan

½ teaspoon poultry seasoning, such as Bell's (it has that rad turkey on it!)

1 garlic clove, minced

1 teaspoon kosher salt, or to taste

3 tablespoons balsamic vinegar

1 teaspoon Dijon mustard

1 teaspoon maple syrup

1 cup Black Bean Hummus (PAGE 163)

4 sub rolls, split lengthwise

2 cups Fritos corn chips (I almost said, "If you can't find Fritos, . . ." but then I remembered that the communists haven't taken over yet!)

4 big romaine lettuce leaves

1 large beefsteak tomato, cut into 8 thin slices

In a large mixing bowl, toss together the chicken, olive oil, poultry seasoning, garlic, salt, vinegar, mustard, and maple syrup. Let the mixture sit for 20 minutes.

Spread some hummus on the top half of each roll. Put some Fritos onto the hummus so that they stick to it and are trapped for all eternity.

Put a quarter of the chicken on the bottom half of each roll. Don't put on too much of the juice from the bowl or your sandwich will get pretty soggy. Top the chicken with lettuce and tomatoes, carefully flip the other half on top, making sure that none of the Fritos are pretending to be stuck and try to escape. Eat!

Roasted Chicken • Canadian Bacon • Pico de Lettuce • Tomatoes • Jalapeño Mayo • BBQ Chips

NO.7 SUB CLUB

Makes 4 subs

Mitch Hedberg would not have let me into his sandwich club with this one. But it is awesome nonetheless, and how can a sub shop make a real club sandwich anyway? Subs are inherently not club sandwiches, but if you can suspend your disbelief, this has all of the ingredients of a club sandwich, just all a little screwed up. And I propose that we put chips on the sandwich.

1 pound Canadian Bacon (PAGE 147), sliced thin

4 sub rolls, split lengthwise

2 cups shredded Roasted Chicken (PAGE 26) or 2 Boneless, Skinless Chicken Breasts (PAGE 27)

½ cup Jalapeño Mayo (PAGE 161)

4 cups BBQ potato chips (see PAGE 183, or, you know, buy them)

2 cups Pico de Lettuce (PAGE 176)

1 large beefsteak tomato, cut into 8 thin slices

Preheat the oven to 400°F.

Lay the Canadian bacon slices out in a single layer on a large baking sheet. Bake for 10 minutes or until hot and slightly caramelized. Put a quarter of the bacon on each of the sliced roll bottoms.

Put a quarter of the chicken on top of the bacon. Put some mayo on each of the bread tops.

Put a quarter of the potato chips on top of the meat on each sandwich. Top with the pico de lettuce and tomatoes and close the sandwiches.

Roasted Chicken • Fried Eggplant • Fresh Mozzarella • Arugula • Special Sauce

THIS IS A CHICKEN SANDWICH

Makes 4 of the best sandwiches you have ever had

I don't eat a ton of meat, and I've thought about becoming a vegetarian many times. But I don't think I ever want to give up eating chicken. Not because I hate chickens and want to prove my dominance over them or anything (because they already know), but because they are the most delicious animals of all time, and if God didn't want me to eat them, he probably wouldn't have made them that way. That said, a lot of people believe that, if you eat the wrong thing or think the wrong thing, God will make you spend eternity bathing in a lake of fire. I'm not sure if I believe in God or not, but I definitely don't believe that God cares about the details of what I eat. Actually, if God really *does* care about what we eat, then it is probably because God isn't super stoked about all of the animals we abuse in factory farms every day, even when we don't have to and there is plenty of broccoli lying around. But I doubt that I will be denied entry into heaven just for eating a few chickens. Right, God??

½ cup Special Sauce (PAGE 163)

4 kaiser rolls, split in half

2 cups shredded Roasted Chicken (PAGE 26) or 2 Boneless, Skinless Chicken Breasts (PAGE 27)

4 large slices Fried Eggplant (PAGE 148)

6 ounces fresh mozzarella, sliced into 4 thick slices

2 loosely packed cups arugula

Put a little sauce on each half of each roll.

Layer ingredients on the sandwiches in the following order: chicken, a slice of eggplant, a slice of mozzarella, arugula.

Curry Chicken Salad • Avocado • Iceberg Lettuce • Fried Squid • Lime Segments

SANDWICHES FALL APART

Makes 4 precious sandwiches

No, the title of this sandwich is not an attempt to impress you with my knowledge of postcolonial literature, but it is in fact a clumsy attempt to point out that curry is a beautiful gift that the rest of the world received from the British Empire in India, even though colonialism was pretty atrocious. Human beings have done some pretty upsetting stuff to each other throughout history and sometimes when I see "Asian Slaw" on a menu it makes me feel like we're not trying hard enough to understand and coexist with other cultures. I only wish I was more educated so that I could say something articulate rather than making a goofy reference to a book that actually has nothing to do with curry. I apologize, but I am drinking as fast as I can so that I can be funny again. I am trying to write "A Heartbreaking Cookbook of Staggering Sandwich Genius," but I realize that it's just "An Immature Food Book of Stuttering Sandwich." Francis? New title? [We're keeping the title. The salespeople like it. —Ed.]

- 3 cups shredded Roasted Chicken (PAGE 26) or 3 shredded Boneless, Skinless Chicken Breasts (PAGE 27)
- 2 teaspoons curry powder
- ½ small red onion, sliced thin
- 2 tablespoons raisins, roughly chopped
- Kosher salt to taste
- 1 tablespoon olive oil
- 2 scallions, sliced thin
- ½ of a very ripe avocado, mashed
- 8 slices of white bread, crusts cut off if you prefer it that way
- 1 recipe Fried Squid (PAGE 157)
- 1 lime, peeled, and segments cut out of the pith, about 2 ounces
- 4 leaves iceberg lettuce

In a medium mixing bowl, combine the chicken, curry powder, red onion, and raisins, and mix well. Season to taste with salt.

Heat the olive oil in a large sauté pan over medium heat. I would use nonstick for this because I'm not afraid of anything. Sauté the chicken, tossing often, to get a little color on it and to toast the curry powder a bit. Don't go crazy here; we like the onions a little undercooked because they are super delicious that way. Put the chicken back into the mixing bowl and add the scallions and avocado and mix thoroughly.

Lay out 4 slices of white bread. Spread the chicken evenly on each piece. Top with the fried squid, lime segments, and a piece of iceberg lettuce. Top the sandwiches with the remaining sliced bread.

SAUSAGES

Texas-Wisconsin Border

Pork & Shrimp Sausage, Roasted Onions, Tomato, Michelada Mayo, Cilantro

•

The Godfather Part II

Chorizo, Ham, Roasted Sweet Potatoes, Muenster, Soppressata, Pickled Jalapeños, Thai Basil

•

The Empire Strikes Back

Grilled Bologna, Garam Masala Corned Beef, Grape & Celery Salad, Russian Dressing

•

Lazaro's Revenge

Chorizo, Scrambled Eggs, Swiss Cheese, Pickled Jalapeños

CLOCKWISE FROM TOP LEFT:

Garlic & Thyme Grilled Bologna, Pork & Shrimp Sausage, Sort-of-Mexican Chorizo

SORT-OF-MEXICAN CHORIZO

Makes about 1½ pounds, enough sausage for all of the people who want fresh chorizo, which is not that many because everybody likes the dry-cured stuff, even though it tastes like messed-up pepperoni

I love fresh Mexican chorizo. It is one of the best sausages, and if you've never had it, don't make this version. Go ahead and get *Charcuterie: The Craft of Salting, Smoking & Curing* and make that version because it is perfect and delicious. Don't get me wrong, this sausage is also delicious, but it's like putting bacon on your first hamburger or pepperoni on your first pizza. Those things taste so different from their original forms, and you should know what the perfect originals taste like. To be honest, I don't understand why anybody would ever put bacon on a hamburger unless they hate the taste of hamburgers and are trying to mask the hamburger with the most aggressive non-hamburger flavor of all time. Francis, agree or disagree? [☹☹☹—Ed.] I sent this recipe to my mom for testing purposes, and she commented that maybe this makes it sound like you shouldn't make this sausage because it's not as good as the Ruhlman one. Betty Kord's words cut like a knife.

2 ounces chipotle chiles in adobo sauce

2 garlic cloves

4½ teaspoons kosher salt

1½ tablespoons white vinegar

1 tablespoon elderflower liqueur

½ of a whole star anise

3 whole cloves

¼ stick cinnamon

1½ pounds ground pork

2 teaspoons finely ground gochugaru (Korean red chile powder) or ancho chile powder

¼ teaspoon sesame oil

Preheat the oven to 400°F.

In a blender, combine the chipotles, garlic, salt, white vinegar, elderflower liqueur, star anise, cloves, and cinnamon, and puree until smooth.

In a medium mixing bowl, combine the ground pork, pureed sauce, chile powder, and sesame oil, and mix aggressively until totally combined.

Spread the pork mixture out on a 13 × 18-inch rimmed baking sheet. Bake for 10 minutes, or until firm to the touch and cooked through.

Once the chorizo is cooled, you can cut this sheet of sausage into shapes appropriate for your sandwich. For the subs that we serve, we cut them into rectangular planks.

GARLIC & THYME GRILLED BOLOGNA

Makes enough for 4 to 8 sandwiches, depending on how much you and your guests like bologna

Bologna doesn't get the credit it deserves. This recipe takes bologna to the next level, but don't think for an instant that I am trying to imply that plain bologna isn't awesome. Bologna has a proud tradition as a German-American sausage, rivaling any other cooked sausage. Mortadella really is just Italian bologna with chunks of lard and pistachios in it, and nobody thinks that's low class. I actually prefer bologna, as it has a softer texture and it's just so happy to be invited to your party.

2 garlic cloves, sliced thin

2 shallots, sliced thin

Pinch of red chile flakes

1 teaspoon sesame oil

2 tablespoons white vinegar

¼ bunch fresh thyme sprigs or 1 teaspoon dried thyme

Zest of 1 orange

2 tablespoons dark brown sugar

2 tablespoons olive oil

2 pounds bologna, sliced into ½-inch rounds (go to a deli counter and ask them to give you the goddamned 2-pound chunk whole and you can slice it yourself ~~(if you wanted an easy book that doesn't swear at you, you could have picked up something by Ina Garten)~~) Francis, why did you cut that line? Do you love her? Is she a Clarkson Potter author?

In a mixing bowl, combine the garlic, shallots, chile flakes, sesame oil, white vinegar, thyme, zest, brown sugar, and olive oil and mix thoroughly. Put the bologna in the bowl and completely coat with the marinade. Let stand for at least 1 hour unrefrigerated or up to 24 hours in the fridge, mixing occasionally to make sure the bologna soaks up the marinade evenly.

Fire up a grill or grill pan; if neither is an option, a large sauté pan slicked with a little vegetable oil will do just fine here. Set the heat to medium high.

Take the bologna out of the marinade and place on the grill or whatever you are working with. If there is still thyme left in the marinade and you are working with an actual grill, pull out the rest of the thyme and place it on top of the bologna. Let the bologna get nice and charred on the first side and then flip and char the other side. It's already cooked, so we're not really worried about an internal temperature here, we just want to get nice grill marks and burn the thyme (chef Greg Brainin of Jean-Georges taught me, among a great many other things, that burned herbs taste like Joey from *Friends*, meaning that it is awesome every once in a while (he didn't use those words)).

If you are doing this in a grill pan or sauté pan, just get nice color on both sides, but don't worry about the thyme thing as it will make your apartment super smoky.

Put the bologna on a plate and brush off any thyme debris.

PORK & SHRIMP SAUSAGE

Makes 1½ pounds, or 12 patties, or enough sausage for a sausage fest, but not in a super masculine way

I really love wonton soup. In fact, I will probably eat some today! Unfortunately, the wontons in my neighborhood are just the regular, big, floppy Americanized wontons. They are totally delicious, but in Chinatown the wontons are little and made with a mixture of pork and shrimp. My favorite ones, at Wonton Noodle Garden on Mott Street, have big chunks of shrimp mixed with the ground pork, and they make my future children smile. I wanted to put the wonton fillings in a sandwich, so I came up with this pork and shrimp sausage. It's also great with eggs really late at night when you're all alone and *Men in Black* is on TV.

½ pound shrimp, any size, peeled and deveined

1 pound ground pork

2 garlic cloves, minced

1 teaspoon ground black pepper

¼ of a whole nutmeg seed, grated

2 tablespoons maple syrup

¼ teaspoon sesame oil

1 tablespoon kosher salt

Vegetable oil, as needed

In a food processor, pulse the shrimp just until chopped (I realize that I just said how much I like the big chunks of shrimp in my wontons, and now I am telling you to puree them in a food processor, but that is because I usually put this sausage in casings, and if you have big chunks it could screw that up (however, you are probably not going to put this sausage into casings because you probably don't have the equipment to do so, so feel free to hand-chop the shrimp so they are chunky!)). Transfer to a mixing bowl.

Add the pork, garlic, pepper, nutmeg, maple syrup, sesame oil, and salt. Mix thoroughly by hand.

At this point the sausage can be formed into 12 2-ounce patties and cooked over medium heat in a sauté pan coated with the oil until cooked through, about 3 to 5 minutes. Or, if you're feeling super confident and have the equipment, you can stuff the sausage into casings and grill it like a boss. Don't get too stressed about this because no matter what you do, people will be like "Pork and shrimp sausage, that's so crazy! Who would have thought?? Genius!!" But then you'll still have to get up and go to work tomorrow and for the rest of your life probably. [☹☹☹ —Ed.]

Pork & Shrimp Sausage • Roasted Onions • Tomato • Michelada Mayo • Cilantro

TEXAS-WISCONSIN BORDER

Makes 4 sandwiches that will confuse the entire states of Texas and Wisconsin

The name of this sandwich is a shout-out to an old family hangout of the same name in Richmond, Virginia. It's got sausage with beer and onions like they do in Wisconsin (sorry it's not a Johnsonville brat, Aunt Barb!), but the beer is in the form of a Michelada Mayo that brings in the Tex-Mex, and it's finished with cilantro just to punctuate the sentence. How clever am I?!?

- Vegetable oil, as needed
- 1 pound Pork & Shrimp Sausage (PAGE 42), sliced open
- 4 Sheboygan hard rolls, split in half (If you're not in Sheboygan, a kaiser roll will work. If you are in Sheboygan, you probably aren't reading this, and if you are, this sandwich probably sounds like a waste of a Sheboygan hard roll.)
- 1 cup Roasted Onions (PAGE 172)
- 1 large beefsteak tomato, cut into 8 thin slices
- ½ cup Michelada Mayo (PAGE 161)
- ½ cup fresh cilantro leaves

Preheat a grill, grill pan, or a large sauté pan over high heat until smoking. Lightly oil the grates of the grill or pan. Sear the already-cooked sausage until hot and charred on both sides. Divide the sausages between the 4 rolls. Top the sausage with the roasted onions, tomatoes, mayo, and cilantro. Close the sandwiches and demolish.

Chorizo • Ham • Roasted Sweet Potatoes • Muenster • Soppressata • Pickled Jalapeños • Thai Basil

THE GODFATHER PART II

Makes 4 subs

Every deli in New York has a sandwich called the Godfather, and it's always just a pile of every kind of meat and cheese that they have. And it's always delicious. The Godfather at Graham Avenue Meats & Deli was particularly great, but we didn't eat enough of them and Graham Avenue Meats & Deli sadly closed.

½ pound ham, sliced thin

4 sub rolls, split lengthwise

1 pound Sort-of-Mexican Chorizo (PAGE 40), cut into 2 × 4-inch planks

1 pound Roasted Sweet Potatoes (PAGE 173)

½ pound Muenster cheese, sliced thin

¼ pound soppressata, sliced thin

½ cup Pickled Jalapeños (PAGE 177)

½ cup lightly packed whole Thai basil leaves

Preheat the oven to 400°F.

I love ham. Put the ham on the bottoms of the bread and add the chorizo followed by the cheese. Put everything, including the tops, on a baking sheet and put it in the oven.

Bake for 10 minutes or until the bread is toasted and the chorizo is hot. Top the tops with the soppressata, pickled jalapeños, sweet potatoes, and basil.

Serve with your hands. Sorry we messed up the jalapeño placement in the photo.

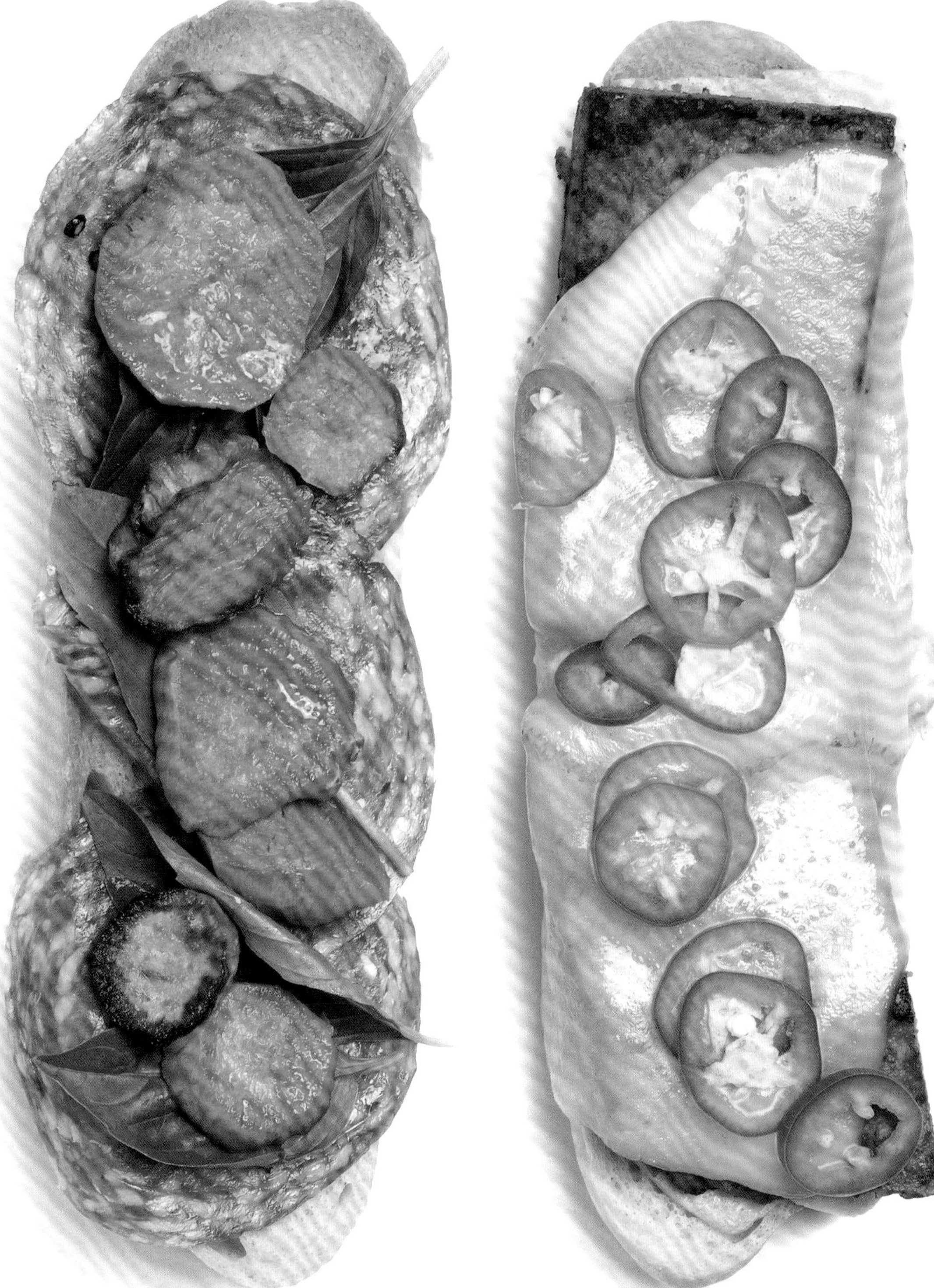

Grilled Bologna • Garam Masala Corned Beef • Grape & Celery Salad • Russian Dressing

THE EMPIRE STRIKES BACK

Makes 4 sandwiches that are so much better than Attack of the Clones

I'm kind of forcing the *Star Wars* theme, but I thought it might give me a better shot at scoring a seat on some kind of panel at Comic-Con on my book tour (Francis, don't worry, I realize that I will have to fund this book tour myself). I have a book deal with ~~Random House~~ Clarkson Potter, and I am still insecure.

- **8 slices pumpernickel/rye swirl (this is important, as it represents Luke's inner struggle between the dark and light sides of the Force)**
- **1 pound Garlic & Thyme Grilled Bologna (PAGE 41) (Han Solo)**
- **1 pound Garam Masala Corned Beef (PAGE 146) (Vader)**
- **2 cups Grape & Celery Salad (PAGE 172) (C3PO)**
- **¼ cup Actual Russian Dressing (PAGE 162) (R2D2)**

Assemble the sandwich with the Force.

Eat the sandwich with the Force.

(If you do want to book me for Comic-Con, please e-mail dreams@no7sub.com)

Chorizo • Scrambled Eggs • Swiss Cheese • Pickled Jalapeños

LAZARO'S REVENGE

Makes 4 breakfast sandwiches that you can eat at any time of the day if you don't have anything better to do

Sometimes I wake up feeling like the worst person in the world. More often I go to bed feeling like the worst person in the world. Look, I know that you're not my therapist. In fact, you are essentially paying me to write this, so if anything, it's more like I should be your therapist, and in that regard I guess I'm not doing a great job. And with this newfound understanding of my role in your universe, let me prescribe this sandwich the next time you are about to go to bed feeling like the worst person ever. It's spicy and meaty and delicious, and it always makes me feel better about things. It helps if you look up at the stars while you eat this sandwich and think about how unfathomably large the universe is and how small your problems must be in the history of the entire, potentially limitless and timeless universe, and then remember that everybody will eventually forget whatever it is that you're stressed out about. Unless you killed a bunch of people on purpose, because they will probably remember that.

- 4 English muffins, split in half
- 4 3 × 3-inch slabs of Sort-of-Mexican Chorizo (PAGE 40)
- 4 slices Swiss cheese
- 4 Perfect Scrambled Eggs (PAGE 155)
- ¼ cup drained Pickled Jalapeños (PAGE 177)

Preheat the oven to 400°F.

Stop. This is spicy, and eating spicy foods before bed makes my dreams super crazy. Either way, go for it, but when you get in bed, after you turn off the light, think really hard about my face while you fall asleep. Then, in the morning, send me an e-mail at dreams@no7sub.com and tell me what I did in your dream. I bet it was awesome!!! (Part of being a good therapist is dream analysis.)

Lay the English muffins, cut side up, on a baking sheet. Put the chorizo on the bottom halves and the Swiss cheese on the tops. Fold in the corners of the cheese so that they don't melt and drip off the English muffin top, or you will have a more difficult time cleaning your baking sheet.

Put the baking sheet in the oven and cook until the cheese is melted, the chorizo is hot, and most importantly, the English muffins are well toasted. Undertoasted English muffins are not nearly as good as perfectly toasted English muffins. (Katherine, please put that on my gravestone if I am not actually immortal.) This should take about 7 to 10 minutes (the English muffins, not dealing with my death, which should take a very, very long time).

Pull the baking sheet out of the oven and top the chorizo with the scrambled eggs and some pickled jalapeños. Sweet dreams!

For the photo, Maggie Ruggiero, my out-of-my-league food stylist, crumbled the chorizo, mixed it with the scrambled eggs and pickled jalapeños, put it on the English muffin, and topped with cheese *before* toasting. She is one of the best people that I know, so I accepted this. And now I don't really like to eat food unless Maggie has styled it first, which is weird and makes mealtimes very difficult.

HEY!
GUEST

BROCCOLI, CAULIFLOWER, ASPARAGUS

Broccoli Classic

Roasted Broccoli, Ricotta Salata,
Lychee Muchim, Pine Nuts

•

ALF

Asparagus, Roasted Tomato Mayo,
Lime, Fried Garlic

•

The #2 Best New Sandwich in America in 2012 According to the *Huffington Post*

Roasted Cauliflower, Smoked French Dressing,
Raisin Relish, Potato Chips

•

Broccoli, Egg & Cheese

Fried Broccoli, Scrambled Eggs,
Smoked Gouda Cheese, Ketchup

I am deeply in love with broccoli on what is a potentially dysfunctional level. Another potential sign of my dysfunction is that when I think about broccoli in gloopy take-out Chinese garlic sauce over rice, I get a little fucked up inside, and then I go and get gnarly drunk in the shower. (The hot water is a perfect contrast for an icy cold beer. (But I have the reflexes of a jungle cat, so you shouldn't try this at home and slip and hit your head. (You should maybe just drink a beer in the bathroom with the shower going so that you can experience the steam vs. cold beer aspect, without the tragic loss of life part.))) And then I go and make a broccoli sandwich.

But all vegetables make excellent sandwiches, and the fact that anybody is ever surprised that I make sandwiches with vegetables for main ingredients is perplexing to me. I'm not sure why some people think that roasted cauliflower is somehow less satisfying than roast beef, but it's that attitude that means that I'll end up having to describe what roast beef tasted like to my grandchildren. Our food system is so broken because of the exaggerated amount of resources required to raise animals quickly enough to feed the zombie hordes that I wouldn't be surprised if wars start over roast beef. I guess maybe people think that society could collapse at any moment, and so they need to eat as much meat as possible to stock up on protein just in case there isn't any for a while. I don't live my life in fear of terrorism or identity theft or any of the horrible things that I can't do anything about, so I live my life as if it is going to go on for one thousand years, and thus I have time for an asparagus sandwich when I feel like it.

ROASTED BROCCOLI OR CAULIFLOWER OR ASPARAGUS

Makes enough for 4 big sandwiches, probably with some left over, but it's good to eat more vegetables

2 heads of broccoli or 1 head of cauliflower or 1 bunch of standard or jumbo asparagus*

2 tablespoons olive or vegetable oil

1 teaspoon kosher salt

* Not the pencil-thin ones, which are delicious and beautiful, but not as fun as bigger asparagus for some reason.

Preheat the oven to 400°F.

For the broccoli: Hold on to the floret end and peel the bottom third of the stem with a vegetable peeler. Then, starting from the stem end, cut ¼-inch rounds, working your way toward the florets. Keep cutting the stem when you get to the florets so that a bunch of them fall away, until you have about 2 inches of broccoli left. Now cut away the florets to separate them and, if any of them are larger than 2 inches at their widest, cut them in half.

For the cauliflower: With a paring knife, trim away all of the florets from the stem. Go through all of the floret pieces and, if any are larger than 2 inches at their widest, cut them in half. Cut off the very bottom of the stem and discard. Peel the stem like you mean it. Now slice the stem into ¼-inch rounds and have a sip of whiskey.

For the asparagus: What is your problem? You're too good for broccoli or cauliflower? You want your pee to smell funny? We actually got several calls to the sub shop, as well as a negative Yelp review, all from this one guy who was convinced that we had done something weird to the asparagus in one of our sandwiches because every time he ate it, his pee smelled bad. We tried to reason with him, but he was upset. Remember that line from *Love in the Time of Cholera*: "Even when it was not the season for asparagus, it had to be found regardless of cost so that he could take pleasure in the vapors of his own fragrant urine."

Trim off the very, very bottom of the asparagus. Now, with a vegetable peeler, peel the bottom 2 inches or so. Cut the asparagus into 1-inch pieces. A long sub sandwich with long, uncut asparagus sounds way cooler than the reality of taking one bite and pulling all of the asparagus out of your sandwich.

Take your vegetable, toss it with oil and salt, and put it on a baking sheet. Roast 15 to 20 minutes for the broccoli and cauliflower, and 10 to 15 for the asparagus. We're looking for caramelized edges, insides somewhat tender, and celebrities calling you to see if you'll endorse their celebrity. Does that make sense? I mean like celebrities hiring *you*, now a more famous celebrity, to promote them as people, because you cook vegetables so perfectly that everybody wants to say they know you.

GRILLED BROCCOLI OR CAULIFLOWER OR ASPARAGUS

Tout dans le leurre est un mensange.
Pardon my French.

- 2 heads of broccoli or 1 head of cauliflower or 1 bunch of standard or jumbo asparagus
- 1 teaspoon kosher salt
- 2 tablespoons olive or vegetable oil

Heat up a grill with the charcoal and the fire and such.

For the broccoli: Quarter the whole head of broccoli lengthwise. Now cut those quarters in half. I could have just said cut the broccoli lengthwise into 8 pieces. Francis, this is why I wish you would return my phone calls. Write something clever here: `[I think either way of expressing this seems fine. —Ed.]`. Ladies and gentlemen, Francis Lam!!!

For the cauliflower: Quarter that beast! Now halve those quarters! I was going to tell you to trim out some of the stem, but I think we should live on the edge on this one. Or I guess this is living a little away from the edge, eating a lot of fiber, and living like healthy people.

For the asparagus: Peel the bottom! Are we not men? You can go Devo or *Island of Dr. Moreau* with that, but know that I'm not trying to be sexist. I'm sorry that this section brings up so many film, literary, and cultural references, but that should clue you in as to how deep a decision you make when you choose a vegetable as your main sandwich component. Pulled pork would be a much less interesting recipe. "Cook some pork. Pull it." See?

Put your chosen vegetable into a pot that is just big enough to hold the vegetable in a single layer on the bottom. Season with the salt and add ½ cup of water for the broccoli and cauliflower, or 2 tablespoons of water for the asparagus. Cook it on high heat, uncovered, until the water boils off; the vegetables should be almost cooked through, about 3 to 5 minutes. If you need a little more time or water, go ahead and add it a tablespoon at a time. If you add too much, it will be okay. I've put too much liquid in my vegetables, *and* I've alienated some of the most important women in New York City, so you'll be fine. Just drain off the excess and adjust the seasoning to taste.

When the veggies are almost cooked, throw them on a baking sheet and let them cool. Toss the vegetables with the oil and transfer them to the grill. They're almost cooked, so this should be quick. You just want to get them nicely charred on the outside, which should only take a few minutes. (If you're grilling asparagus, cut it into bite-size pieces after grilling.) You are going to be so pleased by this, I promise!

Roasted Broccoli • Ricotta Salata • Lychee Muchim • Pine Nuts • Fried Shallots

BROCCOLI CLASSIC

Makes 4 large subs

I have been making broccoli sandwiches for myself since I was a kid. In high school I would sauté broccoli and put it on top of mashed potatoes between two slices of bread. In my early twenties I got hooked on steamed broccoli with ham and cheese on a sesame seed hamburger bun. Now I roast it and top it with mayo, pickled lychees, pine nuts, and a salty, crumbly cheese.

½ cup Mayo (PAGE 160)

4 sub rolls, split lengthwise

2 heads of roasted broccoli (PAGE 56) or grilled broccoli (PAGE 57)

1 cup Lychee Muchim (PAGE 69), mostly drained of its juice

1 cup ricotta salata cheese, shredded like a motherfucker

¼ cup pine nuts, toasted

¼ cup Fried Shallots (PAGE 175)

This one could be hot or cold—it just depends on your confidence level and attitude. If you want it to be hot, I suggest having everything ready so that when you finish cooking the broccoli, you're ready to make a sandwich.

Put some mayo on the rolls and top with the broccoli and lychee muchim. Press it all down a little with your hand so that you make a nice flat base for the cheese, pine nuts, and shallots. Sprinkle on the cheese, pine nuts, and shallots, and close the sandwich.

Asparagus • Roasted Tomato Mayo • Lime • Fried Garlic

ALF

Makes 4 adorable sandwiches

Chefs and the people who talk about food on television are fond of saying that you should find the best, freshest ingredients possible to make the best food. I get so bummed out every time I hear somebody say something so ignorant and destructive. I mean, if everybody is supposed to be looking for the best, freshest ingredients possible, what do these chefs and food personalities think should be done with the ingredients that are neither the best nor the freshest? Throw them all away? I think maybe it would be more productive to teach people how to make food taste great so that the cheap, bruised, slightly past-its-prime asparagus is pretty delicious too. It just needs a little fried garlic, lime juice, olive oil, and salt, and it's going to be awesome. Of course, if you want to be known as an excellent grocery shopper, continue to try to find the worlds' best, freshest tomato, slice it, season it with salt and olive oil, and serve it to your friends. They will undoubtedly be impressed. But if you want to be known as an excellent cook, then you should become a champion of the less-than-perfect ingredient. Make it a point to find food that doesn't look great and turn it into something that transcends itself. *That* is what cooking is all about. Pleasing people. Not pleasing people at the expense of food suppliers and landfills, just pleasing people.

2½ tablespoons salted butter

4 split-top hot dog buns

1 bunch of roasted asparagus (PAGE 56) or grilled asparagus (see PAGE 57)

½ cup Roasted Tomato Mayo (PAGE 169)

1 tablespoon Fried Garlic (PAGE 180), crumbled a little

1 lime, cut into segments for squeezing

Melt the butter in a sauté pan large enough to hold all 4 hot dog buns over medium heat. Dip both sides of each bun in the butter and then let them ride on one side until golden brown. Flip them and get them golden on the other side.

Put some asparagus into each bun, and top with a drizzle of mayo and a sprinkle of fried garlic. Plate each sandwich with a lime wedge on the side for your guests to ignore like it's not a big deal that you are serving lime during a lime price crisis (sorry, I am writing this during a lime price crisis, but hopefully that will be over by the time that you are reading this). Squeeze your lime on your sandwich and know that you still aren't enjoying it as much as your guests because they're generally much happier people than you are.

Roasted Cauliflower • Smoked French Dressing • Raisin Relish • Potato Chips

THE #2 BEST NEW SANDWICH IN AMERICA IN 2012 ACCORDING TO THE *HUFFINGTON POST*

Makes 4 terrible and unhealthy sandwiches

So, a couple of years in a row we got put on this arbitrary list of "Best New Sandwiches in America." Don't get me wrong, I was perfectly thrilled and honored to be included, both times, but really, how can you identify the ten best new anything out of all of the instances of new versions of that thing on this entirely gigantic planet in a whole year and have it be real? You couldn't tell me the ten best new trees on a single block without missing a truly incredible one that everybody but you loves. So I didn't print it out and post it on the wall of the shop, but I appreciated it. But just now, as I was about to start writing the recipe, I decided to look at that article again. And then I read the comments, and they are incredible. People in the world are really angry and jealous, and I totally get it because I am *often* angry and jealous. But some people in the world actually think that other people in the world should *care* that they are angry and jealous. The comments can be broken down into four categories:

1) "These sandwiches all look terrible."

2) "These sandwiches all look terrible and I have a much better idea that involves avocados and onions." (Better sandwich ideas always involve avocados and onions, and often bacon; professional sandwich makers take note!)

3) "How could you leave off Primanti Bros.?" (I just looked at their website and they haven't changed their menu since 1933, so I think you missed the point of "new," but now I want to go to Pittsburgh.)

4) "These sandwiches all look really unhealthy." (But mine is made of fucking cauliflower, which is low in fat and high in folate and vitamin C! (Can't you fucking read?!?! (And fucking raisins for fiber (and French dressing because the French live longer!! (And potato chips because I hate you!!!)))))

I feel like we are all learning a lot about punctuation here. I also have the true secret to happiness on planet Earth: Nobody cares about what you or anyone you know thinks about anything at all, whatsoever. And don't get that twisted; people are paying me to write this stupidity because they actually care what I have to say. But you, Mr. Internet Commenter, are not an expert on sandwiches, and nobody cares what you think about a turkey sandwich with avocados and onions. I'm not trying to be a jerk here, but it's true, and you'll feel better when you accept it. Nobody cares at all what I think about engine configurations, so I don't write about them. "But where is the happiness?" you ask. Well, I lied, because maybe there is no happiness. But "smell the roses" and "42" seem like pretty good answers. And sandwiches are fun, no?

4 sub rolls, split lengthwise

1 head of roasted cauliflower (PAGE 56) or grilled cauliflower (PAGE 57)

1 cup Raisin & Scallion Relish (PAGE 177)

½ cup Smoked French Dressing (PAGE 162)

2 cups Basic Potato Chips (PAGE 182)

Preheat the oven to 400°F.

Place all of the bread, cut side up, on a sheet tray. Pile a quarter of the cauliflower on each of the bottom pieces. Put the tray in the oven and cook for 6 minutes, or until the bread is toasted and the cauliflower is warm.

Top each sandwich with some of the relish, a drizzle of the dressing, a handful of potato chips, and the tops of the rolls.

Fried Broccoli • Scrambled Eggs • Smoked Gouda Cheese • Ketchup

BROCCOLI, EGG & CHEESE

Makes 4 of the best breakfast sandwiches famous chef Nate Appleman has ever had

I am seriously into breakfast sandwiches. And one day chef Nate Appleman came to No. 7 for brunch and had the Broccoli, Egg & Cheese and said that it was the best breakfast sandwich he had ever had. Do you know who Nate Appleman is? First of all, he is a famous chef. Second of all, he is the guy who wins everything on *Chopped* and is trying to figure out how a huge chain restaurant, specifically Chipotle Mexican Grill, can serve meat that isn't killing the world. Talk about a corporate American Sisyphus!!! I love you, Nate Appleman. [Is this going to upset him? Is it going to super upset him? —Ed.] I don't understand. Do you think that my love is so upsetting?

4 English muffins, split in half

4 slices smoked Gouda cheese

4 chunks Fried Broccoli (PAGE 155)

4 Perfect Scrambled Eggs (PAGE 155)

2 tablespoons bottled ketchup*

Preheat the oven to 375°F.

Lay out the muffins on a baking sheet and put a slice of cheese on each of the tops. Fold in the corners of the cheese. Put the baking sheet in the oven and dance to "Easy Lover" by Phil Collins and Philip Bailey exactly two times.

Remove the muffins from the oven and top with broccoli, eggs, and ketchup.

* I will eat homemade ketchup when people figure out how to make artisanal high-fructose corn syrup.

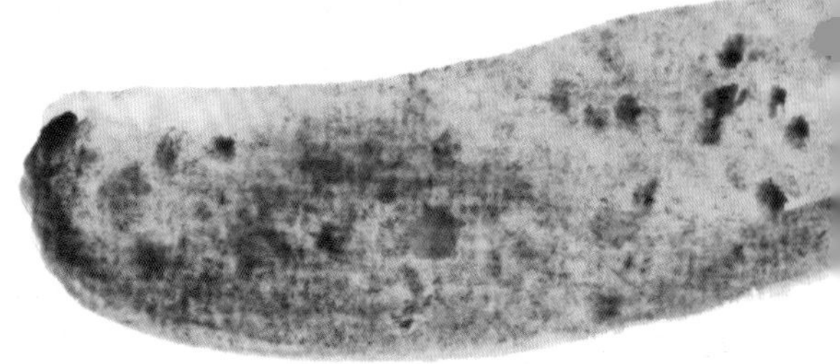

MUCHIM

The Shadiest One

Cheddar, Avocado Ricotta, Cucumber Muchim, Fried Shallots

•

The Suzanne Sugarbaker

Chicken-Fried Mushrooms, Peach Muchim, Mayo

•

Bacon von Braunhut

Shrimp Muchim, Bacon, Granny Smith Apple, Mayo

•

That Time Chris Parnell Played Benedict Arnold on *Drunk History*, the Sandwich

Poached Egg Muchim, Avocado, Onion

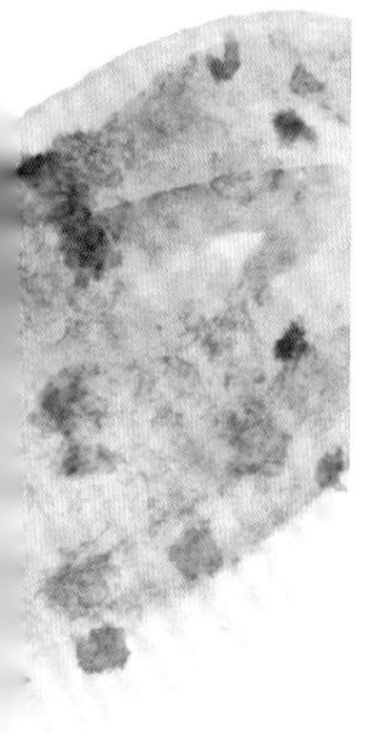

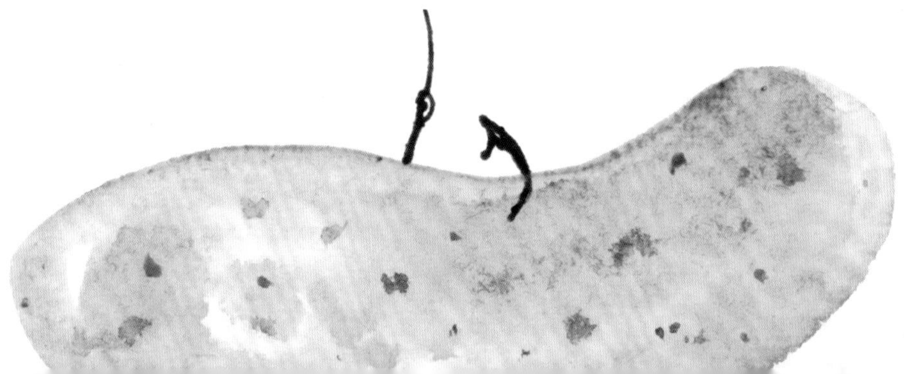

CLOCKWISE FROM TOP RIGHT:

Peach Muchim, Lychee Muchim, Cucumber Muchim, Shrimp Muchim, Tomato Muchim

MUCHIM BRINE

Makes 1 cup of marinade, good for soaking about 2 cups of anything

In Korean, the word *muchim* means "mixed" or "seasoned" but is generally employed to describe a Korean cucumber salad called "*oi muchim.*" It is spicy and intense and tastes a little bit like a fresh (as in nonfermented) kimchi. At No. 7 Sub, I wanted to fuse oi muchim with a classic kosher dill pickle. We use whole Kirby cucumbers and marinate them in the oniony, garlicky brine described below for a few days. And when we decided to try the brine on lychees, it made something super magical! Here is the main recipe for the brine and a few suggestions of what to brine with it, but you should use it for anything that you like to pickle.

1 garlic clove, minced

1 1-inch piece of ginger, peeled and sliced against the grain, then minced

1 medium shallot, finely chopped

A few drops of sesame oil

1 tablespoon sugar

2 teaspoons red chile flakes (this is a pretty spicy recipe, so if you're not into it, maybe just do 1 teaspoon, but keep in mind it is just a small component of a sandwich, so don't take the chiles out entirely or I will know)

1 cup white vinegar

2 whole scallions, thinly sliced

½ tablespoon kosher salt

Stir together the garlic, ginger, shallot, sesame oil, sugar, chile flakes, vinegar, scallions, and salt until thoroughly mixed. This marinade can be used to pickle just about anything. Just soak whatever you'd like in the brine for at least an hour before using, and save it in the brine, refrigerated, for up to a couple of weeks. Here are just a few examples of things that are awesome in this brine:

Cucumber Muchim
Add 2 large cucumbers, sliced into ¼-inch chips.

Lychee Muchim
Drain one 20-ounce can of lychees (save the syrup to make cocktails!), halve them, and combine them with the marinade.

Peach Muchim
Add 4 ripe peaches, pits removed and sliced into ½-inch wedges.

Tomato Muchim
Add 3 large beefsteak tomatoes, cored and cut into ½-inch pieces.

Shrimp Muchim
Peel and devein 1 pound shrimp, slice them in half lengthwise, cook them, and add them to the brine.

Here are some things that would not be super awesome in this brine:

Car Batteries
Do you have a container that big anyway?

Precious Memories
This brine will not preserve things in the way you need it to. Isn't there somebody in your life that you can really talk to?

Cigarettes
Actually, if you wanted to soak your cigarettes in this, and then let them dry out again, I'll bet they would be pretty awesome.

Cheddar • Avocado Ricotta • Cucumber Muchim • Fried Shallots

THE SHADIEST ONE

Makes 4 big, cheesy sandwiches or 8 smaller open-face things

This will be so delicious, and you deserve something delicious. Or maybe you don't. You're not the customer who orders a sandwich, and then upon receiving it, asks for a bag in the rudest way you can possibly muster, are you? We have these customers who get so frustrated because they are not immediately handed a bag (and this is for a single sandwich, already wrapped and sealed in wax paper), and they have to let me know how upset they are. I don't automatically hand out bags because they're unnecessarily wasteful in this situation, but if you want one, then that's on *your* conscience. So just ask! What you do instead is say, "Um, this is *to go*. You didn't give me a *bag*." You are the reason that I started buying tiny, handleless bags, in the hope that upon receiving said bag, you would feel stupid and stop being such a tool. But it turns out that you're quite satisfied with those bags. You don't make any sense. I'm going to start making little handles for your sandwich out of masking tape and make you carry your sandwich like a tiny, broccoli-filled briefcase. And don't make this sandwich because it is too good for you.

1 ripe avocado

1 cup ricotta cheese

1 teaspoon kosher salt

Juice of 1 lemon

8 slices country white bread

8 to 16 slices awesome Cheddar cheese, depending on how much cheese you like

1 cup Cucumber Muchim (PAGE 69)

4 tablespoons Fried Shallots (PAGE 175)

Preheat the oven to 400°F.

In a food processor, combine the avocado, ricotta, salt, and lemon juice and process until smooth.

Lay out the bread on a baking sheet and top with the Cheddar cheese. Bake until the bread is toasted and the cheese is melted, about 6 to 8 minutes. Top the cheese with a schmear of avocado ricotta, some cucumber muchim, and a sprinkle of fried shallots. You can fold the pieces together to make 4 sandwiches, or you can leave them separate for 8 pieces of cheesy toast.

Chicken-Fried Mushrooms • Peach Muchim • Mayo

THE SUZANNE SUGARBAKER

Makes 4 miraculous sandwiches

Chicken-fried steak is made from beef! It's beef!!! I realize that you already knew that, but you'd be amazed by how many people order it and then say, "Um, I ordered the chicken. This doesn't look like chicken." But I don't laugh at them because it *is* a little confusing. Just like when everybody makes fun of the Insane Clown Posse for not knowing how magnets work, because I don't actually know how magnets work. There are lots of reasons to make fun of the Insane Clown Posse, but their honesty and self-understanding about what is beyond their mental grasp is frankly great, and I wish we all had the courage to admit what we don't understand. Also, pickled peaches and fried things go so well together that dogs can hear your pleasure at an octave we can't even perceive. Miracles!

And this isn't chicken-fried steak anyway, it's mushrooms.

- 8 slices Wonder bread
- ½ cup Mayo (PAGE 160)
- 8 pieces Chicken-Fried Mushrooms (PAGE 149)
- ½ cup Peach Muchim (PAGE 69)

Lay out all of the bread and spread mayo on one side of each piece.

Put 2 pieces of mushroom on 4 slices of bread and top each with the peach muchim. Close the sandwiches and cut them in half diagonally.

BACON VON BRAUNHUT

Makes 4 sandwiches

Shrimp is a really challenging thing. There are very few shrimp that are okay to eat, ethically speaking. They're either a part of the destruction of ecosystems when farmed, part of the depletion of fish in the ocean when they're fished, part of the reason that slave labor still exists, or all of the above. So maybe swap out the shrimp in this recipe for a nice mackerel fillet.

But if you have shrimp, then maybe think about where it comes from. Go to a fishmonger and talk to him or her about it. The domestic stuff is your best bet, because it's wild and still abundant, and you avoid the slave labor stuff. And then put bacon on it and everybody will forget all about it.

I know, you're wondering why I even put shrimp in this book if I think it is so terrible. The thing is that I *love* shrimp, and I just want us all to think about it a little more and maybe eat a lot less of it so that it can exist longer, so when we do occasionally eat it, we can feel better about it.

¼ pound bacon, cut into ½-inch pieces

4 split-top hot dog buns

½ cup Mayo (PAGE 160)

2 cups Shrimp Muchim (PAGE 69), drained

1 Granny Smith apple

Put the bacon in a sauté pan large enough to hold all 4 of the hot dog buns, but don't put in the buns. Cook the bacon over medium heat for 8 to 10 minutes, or until the bacon fat is well rendered and the bacon is crisp but not totally dried out. With a slotted spoon, remove the bacon and reserve it in a small bowl lined with a paper towel. Pour the bacon fat into a heatproof bowl.

Dip both sides of each bun in the bacon fat and then let them ride on one side in the pan over medium heat until golden brown. Flip them and get them golden on the other side.

Put some mayo into each of the buns. Divide the shrimp between the 4 buns. Using a Japanese mandoline with the little julienne teeth set into it, cut the apple, being careful not to use the core and also being careful not to cut off part of your hand. Maybe use that guard thingy that came with the mandoline. And if you're sitting there feeling sad that you don't have a mandoline, just cut them by hand. Top the sandwiches with some apples and the bacon!

Poached Egg Muchim • Avocado • Onion

THAT TIME CHRIS PARNELL PLAYED BENEDICT ARNOLD ON *DRUNK HISTORY*, THE SANDWICH

Makes 2 sandwiches

This sandwich sounds so awesome that I refuse to even test it. Francis, this recipe is untested. "Daring" you say? "Stupid and irresponsible"? [That's stupid and irresponsible. —Ed.] Well, I am in charge of my own destiny, and I refuse to make this sandwich because I will bet the house on the fact that it is so, so good! There is enough vinegar in the brine to poach a beautiful egg and enough salt to make it delicious. And avocado and onions win every time! I'm still listening to "Easy Lover" from the last recipe I wrote, and I feel like Phil Collins would want me to let this one ride. And I know what Philip Bailey would say! But I can't print it because this *is* a family book.

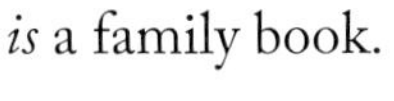

1 recipe Muchim Brine (PAGE 69)

2 eggs

2 English muffins, split in half

½ ripe avocado, sliced

4 perfect, thin slices of a red onion

Seriously, get ready for this. We are making cookbook history in that you are doing a recipe that has never been tested!† It might be terrible! Actually, I'll bet that a lot of recipes are never tested, and maybe that's why Mark Bittman ruined one of my first dinner parties ever by telling me that I could roast a 3- to 4-pound chicken in 40 minutes. I would like to officially thank everybody who came to my *How to Cook Everything* party in Greenpoint in 2001 for their patience and understanding. [We publish Mark, and whether he is helping readers cook simple, delicious, healthful meals or offering commentary on the most important food politics or health issues of our time, his books are excellent. (We didn't publish *How to Cook Everything*, though. For complaints regarding that title, please contact Houghton Mifflin Harcourt.) —Ed.] Thanks for having my back, Francis. And for the record, I think Mark Bittman is totally awesome, and I have tons of imaginary conversations with him regarding my own concerns on eating meat vs. not eating meat. I just think that he has a fancy convection oven and I almost served medium-rare chicken to a bunch of friends who to this day probably still think it's weird that I'm a chef.

Preheat the oven to 400°F. If you have a toaster you can skip this step. I am a minimalist, so I don't buy into the consumerist ideology that I need a toaster.

In a small pot, bring the muchim brine to a boil and then reduce the heat to low so that the water is steaming but not bubbling. Crack your eggs into the brine. Maybe do an extra one or two just in case you screw this up. Let the eggs poach, gently stirring once to make sure they don't stick to the bottom, for about 4 minutes. We want them a little firm so they aren't too messy.

Meanwhile, toast your English muffins until crispy and brown and triumphant.

With a slotted spoon, remove the eggs, shake off the brine, and put them onto the English muffin bottoms. Top with some avocado and onion. Put the tops on and take a picture and Instagram it with the hashtag #whatisasandwich.

† Okay, I did end up having to make this sandwich for the photo, but I did it with my eyes closed, so it's still essentially untested.

FRIED THINGS WITH GOOEY SAUCES

The Battle of Shanghai

General Tso's Tofu, Spaghetti Squash Salad, Pickled Ginger, Shiso, Mayo

•

The Battle of Puebla

General Ignacio's Chicken, Roquefort, Pickled Red Onions, Cilantro

•

The Battle on Pork Chop Hill

General Ruffner's Fried Soft-Boiled Egg, Cucumber Muchim, Blue Cheese

•

Famous Rap Battles of History

General Tso's Fried Fish, Cole Slaw, Dirty Tartar Sauce

CLOCKWISE FROM BOTTOM RIGHT:

*General Tso's Sauce, General Clark L. Ruffner ****'s Sauce, General Ignacio's Sauce*

GENERAL TSO'S SAUCE

Makes about 2 cups of sauce, enough to coat stuff for 8 to 12 sandwiches

To be honest, I never loved General Tso's chicken. But I've always been fascinated by it. It's a perfect example of the notion that traditions are still evolving. It is in no way a traditional Chinese dish, but somehow it is on the menu of every single Chinese restaurant in America, and so it has become a new tradition.

So one day in early 2010, just before service when we were about to start serving a new fried catfish sandwich, I suddenly changed my mind and decided that it should be a General Tso's catfish sandwich instead. I asked my sous chef, who goes by Gabriel Llanos, to make a General Tso's sauce. He made this awesome sauce that then went on to become the sauce for a General Tso's tofu sandwich, which has made a lot of people happy. He never got much credit for the work he did for me, but he is incredibly talented, and this cookbook probably wouldn't exist without his hard work. Every time I think of him, I hear the song "Heaven Is a Place on Earth," but in the kitchen it always went, "Ooh, heaven is not for Gabe." Not because he worships the devil or anything, just because heaven is for dudes helping each other out and playing online poker.

Francis, I know that doesn't make a ton of sense and that I shouldn't waste space on inside jokes, but Gabe is going to laugh a lot when he reads that. I'm pretty drunk now. Apologies. [Wait, should I be cutting out all the parts where you either say you're drunk and/or are obviously writing while drunk? —Ed.]

1 tablespoon cornstarch

1 1-inch chunk of ginger, peeled, sliced into thin rounds

4 garlic cloves

½ cup kecap manis (sweet soy sauce) or molasses with a pinch of salt

½ cup white vinegar

½ cup white wine (really any white wine will do)

2 teaspoons sesame oil

1 teaspoon red chile flakes

½ cup low-sodium soy sauce

In a blender, combine the cornstarch, ginger, garlic, kecap manis, vinegar, wine, sesame oil, red pepper, and soy sauce and puree until smooth. Immediately transfer it to a saucepan and bring just to a boil over medium-high heat, whisking constantly; it will thicken a bit when it comes to a boil. Transfer the sauce to a container to cool down.

GENERAL IGNACIO'S SAUCE

Makes about 2 cups, enough to coat stuff for 8 to 12 sandwiches

This is the General Tso's equivalent of a mole poblano. This is absolutely not a mole poblano, so everybody can calm down. I watched Holland beat Mexico in the World Cup today, and I am not trying to add insult to injury here. I hate soccer because it is the worst sport ever, but I still felt horrible when, after the game, one of my favorite cooks/people named Lazaro had to go to the bathroom and cry (see his sandwich on page 50). That said, Lazaro thinks this sauce is awesome.

1½ tablespoons canola oil

1 tablespoon ancho chile powder

½ tablespoon finely ground gochugaru (Korean red chile powder) or ancho chile powder

¼ teaspoon ground black pepper

2 whole cloves

½ stick of cinnamon

2 plum tomatoes, halved

½ medium yellow onion, quartered

2 garlic cloves

¼ of a 7-ounce can of chipotle chiles in adobo sauce

¼ cup pecans, roughly chopped and lightly toasted

1 teaspoon tahini

½ ounce dark chocolate

1 tablespoon white vinegar

1 tablespoon lime juice

½ tablespoon maple syrup

2 teaspoons kosher salt

Preheat the broiler.

In a large saucepan over low heat, cook 1 tablespoon of canola oil, the ancho chile powder, Korean red chile powder, black pepper, cloves, and cinnamon, stirring constantly until nicely toasted and very aromatic, about 3 to 4 minutes. It will form a very thick paste.

In a mixing bowl, combine the tomatoes, onion, garlic, and the remaining ½ tablespoon of oil and toss. Spread out on a baking sheet and put under the broiler to cook until the top is nicely burnt, about 10 minutes. The tomato skins will turn black, the edges of the onions will become a dark brown that is almost black, and the tops of the garlic should also be super dark brown, but not quite black. Transfer to the pot with the spices and stir.

Add the chipotles, pecans, tahini, dark chocolate, vinegar, lime juice, maple syrup, and salt, increase the heat to medium low, and continue cooking, stirring occasionally, until your apartment smells awesome and people stop texting you trying to get you to do things you don't want to do. Actually, just cook the mixture for about 10 minutes. People will literally always want you to do things you don't want to do, so just pour yourself a drink, put your phone on "Do Not Disturb," and then smash it with a medium sauté pan, being careful not to get bits of metal and plastic into the sauce, until completely obliterated, 1 to 3 minutes.

Pour the contents of the pot carefully into a blender and puree until smooth. The sauce should be thick but still nice and spreadable.

GENERAL CLARK L. RUFFNER ****'S SAUCE

Makes about 2 cups of sauce, enough to coat stuff for 8 to 12 sandwiches

The people of Buffalo, New York, have a long and proud tradition of frying chicken wings and then making them soggy in one of the most delicious ways possible. I grew up in Ithaca, New York, a town that is an hour closer to the First Niagara Center than it is to Madison Square Garden. And I grew up with a healthy appreciation for buffalo wings. This sauce won't take you back to the Anchor Bar, but you could just look up that recipe on the Internet if that's what you really want. Unless, of course, you're reading this book in some postapocalyptic future, in which case you are going to have a very screwed-up idea of food history if this is your only cookbook.

4 tablespoons (½ stick) unsalted butter, cut into 4 pieces

1½ garlic cloves, roughly chopped

1½ fresh long red chiles, such as cayenne peppers or red finger chiles, stems removed, chopped

1 red bell pepper, stems and seeds removed, finely chopped

½ tablespoon gochujang*

½ tablespoon honey

½ cup white vinegar

A few drops of sesame oil

1 teaspoon kosher salt

In a medium saucepan, melt 2 chunks of the butter over low heat. Once it is completely melted, increase the heat to medium, add the garlic, and sweat it while stirring for 2 minutes, or until it just begins to brown. Add the chiles and bell peppers and continue to cook until everything is super soft and melty, but the peppers aren't caramelized, about 10 minutes.

Pour the stew into a blender, add the gochujang, honey, vinegar, sesame oil, and salt, and puree until smooth.

If you're going to use the sauce now, return it to the pot and add the rest of the butter over low heat, a piece at a time, stirring until it's completely melted and incorporated. If you're not going to use it now, cool the sauce as is, and reheat and add the butter when you are ready to use it.

* It's a Korean fermented chili and soy bean paste that tastes like miso that can't be bothered to give a fuck. That's a good thing.

General Tso's Tofu • Spaghetti Squash Salad • Pickled Ginger • Shiso • Mayo

THE BATTLE OF SHANGHAI

Makes 4 more tofu sandwiches than you've probably ever eaten in your life

General Tso's Sauce with fried tofu is excellent, but then again, most things with fried tofu are awesome. Unless you're worried about plant estrogen . . . but why worry?

- 2 cups Spaghetti Squash Salad (PAGE 178)
- 4 sub rolls, split lengthwise
- ½ cup Mayo (PAGE 160)
- 1 pound Fried Tofu, cut in 8 pieces (PAGE 151)
- 1 cup General Tso's Sauce (PAGE 82)
- 2 tablespoons sesame seeds (preferably mixed black and white for pizazz and equality)
- ¼ cup pickled ginger (the pink one will look cooler on the sandwich)
- 8 shiso leaves (if you can't find fresh shiso, use mint)

Put a quarter of the spaghetti squash on each of the bread bottoms and put a little mayo on each of the tops.

While the tofu is still hot, put it in a bowl and add the General Tso's sauce. Toss everything around and get it all saucy. Sprinkle with the sesame seeds, and place 2 pieces of tofu on each sandwich. Top with a little pickled ginger, and place 2 leaves of shiso on each sandwich before putting on the tops.

General Ignacio's Chicken • Roquefort • Pickled Red Onions • Cilantro

THE BATTLE OF PUEBLA

Makes 4 sandwiches

Because our General Ignacio's Sauce is so thick and awesome, we don't need to bread the chicken in a particularly fancy way. And you can use white or dark meat, knowing that the dark meat is a little more flavorful but also a little more chewy, and the white meat is a little less forgiving of overcooking but more tender and pretty. The choice is yours!

- **1 quart vegetable or canola oil, for frying**
- **1 pound boneless, skinless chicken, cut into 1-inch chunks**
- **Kosher salt**
- **½ cup all-purpose flour**
- **1 cup General Ignacio's Sauce (PAGE 83)**
- **8 slices from a round loaf of rustic, crusty French bread**
- **½ cup Roquefort (you can use any crumbly blue cheese here, but Roquefort fits with the theme!)**
- **½ cup Pickled Red Onions (PAGE 173)**
- **½ cup fresh cilantro leaves**

In a large saucepan, heat the oil to 400°F over medium-high heat. (Use a deep-fry thermometer.)

In a medium mixing bowl, toss the chicken pieces with 1 teaspoon of salt. Let the chicken absorb the salt for 5 minutes, and then add the flour and mix to coat the chicken thoroughly.

In a small saucepan, heat the General Ignacio's sauce on low heat until warm.

When the oil is ready, carefully add the chicken one piece at a time. Cook them in small batches, making sure there's plenty of room between each piece. Fry the chicken until just cooked through and golden brown on the outside, 4 to 6 minutes per batch. Transfer to paper towels and let it rest, sprinkling a little more salt on top.

Toast the bread and lay it all out. Sprinkle a thin layer of cheese onto each piece of bread.

In a clean mixing bowl, toss the cooked chicken with the General Ignacio's sauce. Put a quarter of the chicken on 4 of the laid-out bread slices. Top with some pickled red onions and cilantro. Close the sandwiches and cut them in half like you are fancy.

General Ruffner's Soft-Boiled Fried Egg • Cucumber Muchim • Blue Cheese

THE BATTLE ON PORK CHOP HILL

Makes 4 sandwiches

Eggs are one of the best foods. I like them for breakfast, but I love them for dinner. This sandwich is going to make your heart explode. Seriously, in all of the ways you can think of.

- 1 cup General Clark L. Ruffner ****'s Sauce (PAGE 84)
- 4 Soft-Boiled Fried Eggs (PAGE 152)
- 4 hamburger buns
- ½ cup Cucumber Muchim (PAGE 69), drained
- ¼ cup crumbled blue cheese

In a small saucepan, heat the General Ruffner's sauce over low heat until warm.

When the eggs are fried and drained, put them in a mixing bowl with the sauce and gently stir to coat them without breaking them.

Open the hamburger buns and put some muchim on the bottoms.

On a cutting board, quickly cut the eggs in half lengthwise and place them on top of the muchim. Make sure that as soon as you cut them completely in half, you turn them up so that the yolks don't run everywhere. This is going to be messy but completely worth it.

Top the sandwiches with a little blue cheese and the tops of the buns, and attack. I realize I just used blue cheese on two sandwiches in a row.

General Tso's Fried Fish • Cole Slaw • Dirty Tartar Sauce

FAMOUS RAP BATTLES OF HISTORY

Makes 4 huge sandwiches

When I was a kid we used to drive up to Skaneateles, New York, to look at the beautiful lake and eat at Doug's Fish Fry. Their sandwiches are so beautiful! It's a huge fish fillet on a tiny bun, and I want to eat it right now.

I think a fried-fish sandwich is in my top-five favorite sandwiches.

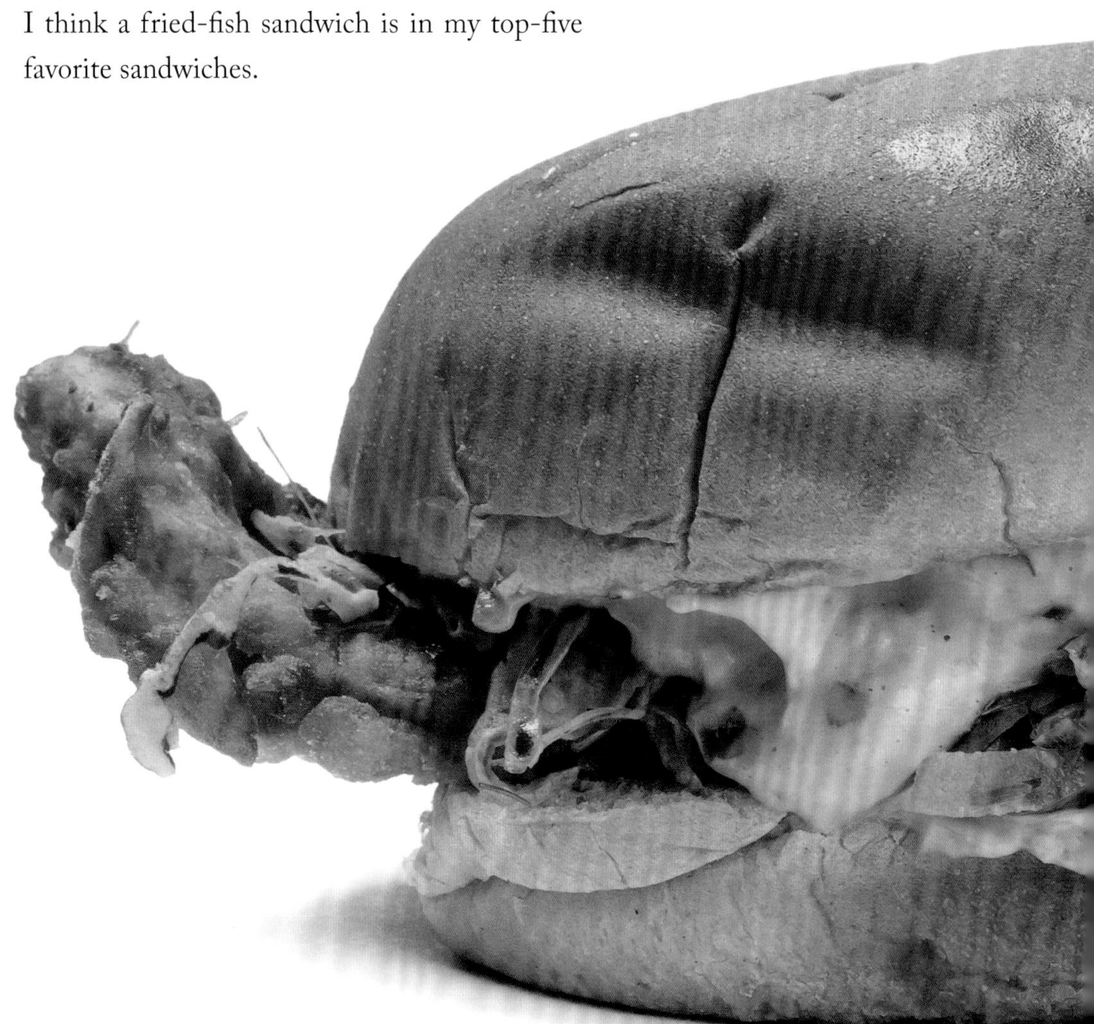

4 pieces Fried Fish (PAGE 152)

1 cup General Tso's Sauce (PAGE 82)

½ cup Dirty Tartar Sauce (PAGE 169)

4 hamburger buns

2 cups Coleslaw (PAGE 181)

In a mixing bowl (or maybe even better yet would be a roasting pan so that you have a flat surface to work with) gently coat the fried fish with the General Tso's sauce, being careful not to break the fish.

Spread some tartar sauce on the hamburger buns and add a piece of fish and some coleslaw to each.

SEAFOOD EXPLOSION

Operation Cornerstone

Poached Arctic Char, Haricots Verts Salad, Fried Garlic, Butter

•

Tyler Kord on Cuyler Gore

Grilled Squid & Zucchini, Green Olives, Red Onions, Fort Greene Goddess Dressing

•

JCVD

Mussels, Brussels Sprouts, Old Bay Curry Sauce, Fresh Mozzarella

•

Mi Corazón Llora

Ceviche, Hummus, Jicama Salad, Leche de Tigre Mayo

FROM LEFT TO RIGHT:

Grilled Squid & Zucchini, Ceviche, Poached Fish, Goldfish

POACHED FISH

Makes enough for 4 sandwiches

Poaching fish is for winners and heroes. Poaching fish keeps it tender, and it makes a super-flavorful broth. If you wanted to make this fish as part of a plate of food, I would recommend that you take the fish out of the poaching liquid once it's cooked, and then return the pan to the heat, reduce the liquid by half, add a little heavy cream and some parsley, and pour it over the fish. Serve it with some roasted potatoes and rock out with your fish out. But we're making sandwiches so we're not going to do that today. But you could also keep the liquid and do that tomorrow. Or cook other stuff in the liquid and you'll have a fish soup. But without the actual fish, because you're putting it on a sandwich first, hero.

You could use just about any kind of fish for this, but arctic char is awesome. It has a nice flavor that is somewhere between that of trout and salmon. And it's a relatively sustainable choice because it is farm raised in pools that aren't connected to the ocean, meaning that it won't pollute anything, and that makes people happy!

2 tablespoons white wine

2 tablespoons olive oil

Zest of 1 lemon

1 teaspoon kosher salt

½ jalapeño, seeds removed

1 piece star anise

½ red onion, sliced thin

¼ cup roughly chopped cilantro leaves (stems reserved)

1 pound arctic char, skin and bones removed, cut into 1-inch cubes

1 tablespoon Fried Shallots **(PAGE 175)**

Preheat the oven to 250°F.

In a small saucepan, combine the wine, 1 cup water, olive oil, lemon zest, salt, jalapeño, star anise, red onion, and cilantro stems, and boil for 5 minutes on high heat.

Place the fish in a saucepan large enough to hold the char in one layer, and, using a wire-mesh strainer, strain the poaching liquid over the fish and discard the solids.

Put the pan in the oven and let poach for 5 minutes. The fish should be just almost cooked through. I would err on the side of undercooked, assuming that you have super-fresh fish. Pour off the excess liquid; add the chopped cilantro, fried shallots, and a little more salt to taste; and very gently stir until everything is mixed together.

CEVICHE

Makes 1 pound, enough for 4 sandwiches. But since the fish doesn't really "cook down" in this preparation, this recipe will make about as much ceviche as you put into it, just like your job, or parenting.

They say that ceviche is from Peru. This recipe for ceviche has nothing to do with Peru, other than saying "ceviche" sounds way better than calling it "acid-cured fish," so I say "ceviche," and Peru will have to come to terms with that. If anything, I'm saying, "Nice fucking word, Peru!" Anyway I think Peru shouldn't worry about what I call ceviche, because Peru should be thinking about their french fries. French fries seem to be the basis of Peru's cuisine, but I didn't have a single good french fry the entire time I was there. But I've stirred up enough trouble with Peru.

Use super-fresh fish, be it fluke, arctic char, or striped bass. It's not super important which because they're all delicious. I really dig Spanish mackerel because it's super sustainable, tender as my ego, and oily and delicious as all get-out.

1 pound boneless, skinless fish fillet (Nobody complains about boneless, skinless fish fillets the way they do about boneless, skinless chicken breasts.)

1 cup lemon juice (from 4 to 6 lemons)

2 cups white vinegar

Kosher salt

1 cucumber, peeled

½ red onion

1 garlic clove, finely chopped

1 tablespoon Fried Shallots (PAGE 175)

A few drops of sesame oil

2 cups apple cider

If you bought filleted fish, check and make sure there are no bones. If you have a whole fish, then you should just throw it in the oven and not get involved in this because it would be hard to explain filleting all of the different shapes of fish, and I'm not getting paid enough to do that. That said, I'm sure they paid Alice Waters plenty to do *In the Green Kitchen*, so why don't you go to page 99 of her book for a pretty straightforward description. Remove the skin and cut the fish into ½-inch pieces and put them in a bowl.

Pour over the lemon juice and vinegar and a few healthy pinches of salt, and mix everything up good. (See, Peru, I know that you're pissed about the lemon juice–vinegar combo. I know that you have some special lime that is the only acid that can be used for ceviche. Well, we don't have that lime, and if it was so good in the first place, then why has nobody else heard of it?)

Let the mixture sit for 10 minutes while you chop the cucumber and onion into tiny pieces.

Strain the fish and put it in a mixing bowl with the cucumber, red onion, garlic, fried shallots, sesame oil, and apple cider (don't even say shit, Peru!) and season generously with salt to taste.

I'm not at your house, but this is delicious and you know it.

GRILLED SQUID & ZUCCHINI

Makes enough for 4 sandwiches

Grilling squid and zucchini together is like grilling peppers and onions together, except that this is squid and zucchini. And just like peppers and onions, grilled squid and zucchini is excellent on its own or on top of Italian sausage. That said, make sure that your squid is not the product of slave labor. How can you tell? Well, if it's frozen and comes from the South Pacific, you may want to be concerned. As with anything, if it's cheap, then there is a reason it is cheap. And we are a huge part of the problem, because when we think it is outrageous to pay more than $10 for fried calamari at a restaurant, that restaurant is going to find a cheaper way to sell you calamari. I'm sorry, I don't mean to make you feel bad. Sandwich time!

2 tablespoons olive oil

2 garlic cloves, chopped fine

1 teaspoon apple cider vinegar

2 teaspoons kosher salt

1 tablespoon honey

1 teaspoon gochujang (Korean chile paste)

12 ounces whole squid, guts, beaks, and eyes removed*

1 large or 2 small zucchini, stems removed, quartered lengthwise into spears

* Peeling the skin is optional; it doesn't really affect the flavor, just the appearance, and if it was removed before you bought it, that's totally fine.

Get a grill super-crazy hot, like the heat from two blazing suns.

In a small mixing bowl, combine the olive oil, garlic, vinegar, salt, honey, and gochujang.

In your chosen vessel, toss the squid and zucchini with the marinade. Let it sit, unrefrigerated, for at least 20 minutes or up to an hour.

Put everything on the grill, and don't worry if you splash some of the marinade onto the coals. We're grilling because we want to burn things on purpose, so feel good about it. Leave the squid and zucchini alone until they look like they're cooked through on one side, about 3 minutes. At this point the squid should be cooked, and if it's opaque, give it a quick flip to cook the top side and then remove it from the grill. The zucchini will need to be flipped and stay on for another 2 to 4 minutes, until nicely charred. Remove the zucchini from the grill.

Once it is cool enough to touch (and by that I mean still pretty hot—no whining; cooking is serious business!), cut the squid into 1-inch ribbons and the zucchini into 1-inch pieces and mix the two things together like they are friends. But they're only friends, and they'll never be more than friends, and that's fine, even though they were clearly meant for each other, but for whatever reason the squid just can't see what is right in front of its eyes. Wait, we removed its eyes, didn't we? Well, you get the point.

Poached Arctic Char • Haricots Verts Salad • Fried Garlic • Butter

OPERATION CORNERSTONE

Makes 4 subs or you didn't follow this recipe

This is a little bit like a tuna salad sandwich, but we're going to use a different fish. I know that in a different part of this book I said to eat all of the tuna until they're extinct [I think we took that part out because it was too weird. —Ed.], but is that what you really want? Look, the seafood section of this book is a little bit heavy, because the decision to eat seafood is kind of heavy. Either you spend a lot of money on it or you buy a product that actually may have ruined people's lives. We used to have a fried clam sandwich on the menu at No. 7 Sub. We used littleneck clams, which are small, delicious, local to New York, and as sustainable as a thing can be. They cost 35 cents each and we put twelve of them on a sandwich. It also had pickled strawberries, roasted leek mayo, and frisée, and we charged $9 for it. People were outraged by the price. Our food cost on the sandwich was around $6. A restaurant's costs break down roughly to 30 percent for staff; 30 percent for food; 10 percent for rent; 10 percent for utilities, insurance, etc.; and the remaining 10 to 20 percent should be profit. So basically, we were paying the customers about $7 to eat that clam sandwich. I know, I am stupid.

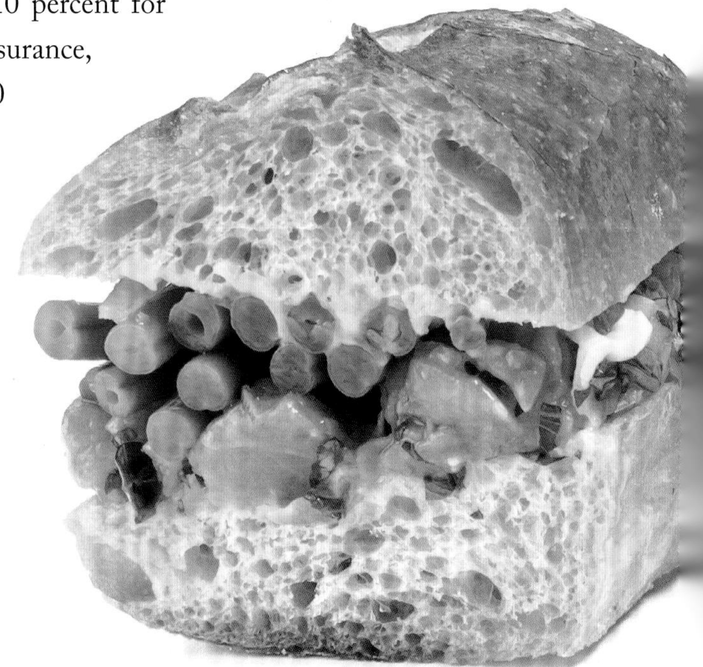

½ stick salted butter, room temperature [If we call this "4 tablespoons" people will be less freaked out. —Ed.] Or we could call it reality. People, it's not the butter that is killing you! It's your inability to make changes in your life! Or maybe it's a velociraptor if you live in Jurassic World, but it probably isn't the butter.

4 sub rolls, split lengthwise

1 pound Poached Fish (PAGE 96)

1 cup Haricots Verts Salad (PAGE 178)

4 teaspoons Fried Garlic (PAGE 180)

Butter the cut side of the rolls and top with fish, haricots verts, and fried garlic. I know exactly what you're thinking. You're thinking that this should be on crustless white bread cut into two precious triangles. Feel free to make this sandwich on crustless white bread cut into two precious triangles. At the end of the day, all I want is for everybody to be happy so that I can get drunk and then go to sleep without having to worry about anybody.*

* I love you.

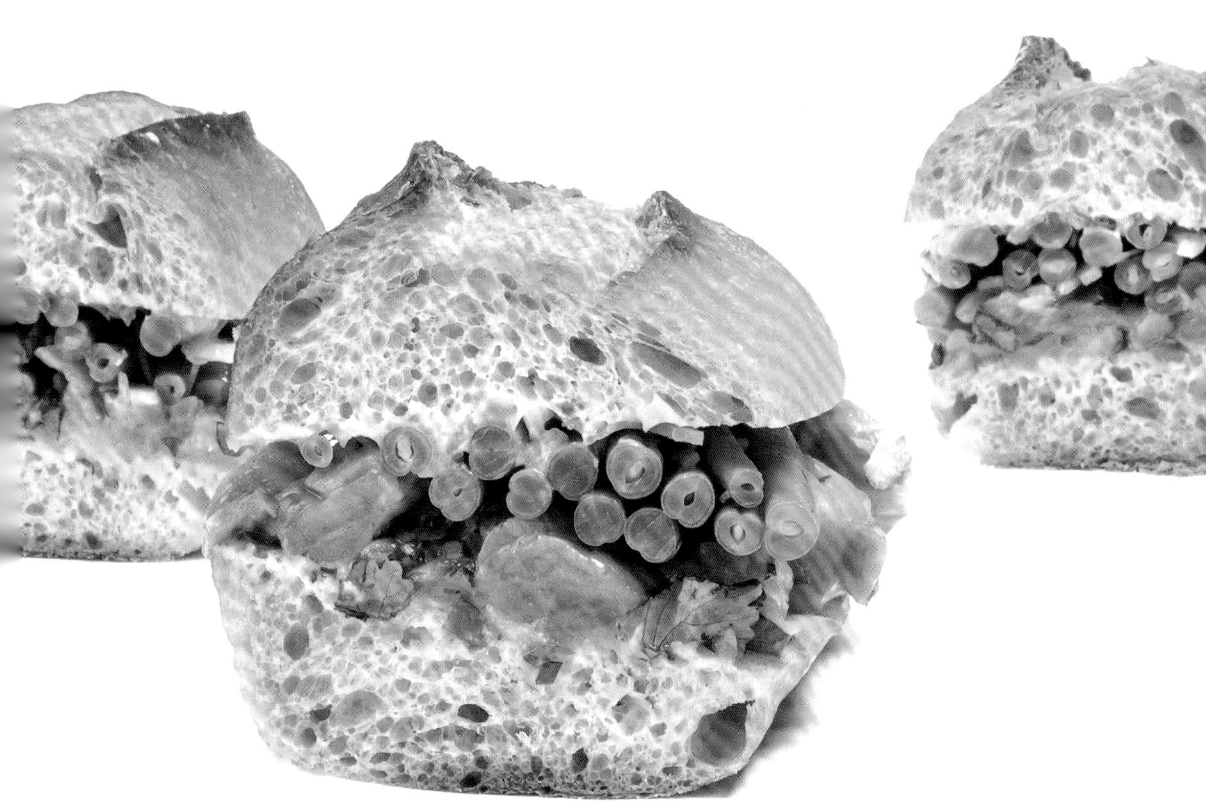

Grilled Squid & Zucchini • Green Olives • Red Onions • Fort Greene Goddess Dressing

TYLER KORD ON CUYLER GORE

Makes 4 subs

This is such a perfect sandwich for summertime! Grilled seafood makes me think about being at the beach and people pulling seafood straight from the ocean so that they can grill it for me. That said, I've never been able to figure out where they actually do that. I've been to Cape Cod, Long Island, Mexico, and Costa Rica, and even at nice restaurants in those places, I've still eaten the same old frozen shrimp and flounder fillets. The closest I've come to that mythic experience was watching a cook receive a fish directly from a fisherman at a restaurant in Rome, Italy, where I trailed for a night. The cook proceeded to fillet and then cook that fish for about thirty minutes longer than it needed to be cooked, and I guarantee that it didn't taste as good as a frozen fish I had once that was thawed, left in a refrigerator for three days, and then seasoned and cooked perfectly at a place in Tulum, Mexico. I ate *that* fish with great relish and appreciation while the sun set and I drank mezcal. Tulum is one of the most wonderful places I've ever been. Cuyler Gore is the name of the park across the street from my restaurant. It's not as nice as Tulum.

1 recipe Grilled Squid & Zucchini (PAGE 98)

½ small red onion, sliced into ¼-inch half-moons

½ cup pitted green olives, sliced into ¼-inch rounds

4 sub rolls, split lengthwise

½ cup Fort Greene Goddess Dressing (PAGE 164)

While the squid and zucchini are grilling, toss the red onion with the olives in a small mixing bowl.

After you've removed your squid and zucchini from the grill and while you are waiting for them to cool a little, put the buns on a cooler part of the grill to toast a bit. When they're warm on the outside, drizzle some dressing inside of them. That sounded gross, and I apologize. Then add the chopped squid and zucchini, and top with the onions and olives. It would not be a terrible idea to have some extra lemon wedges around for squeezing.

Mussels • Brussels Sprouts • Old Bay Curry Sauce • Fresh Mozzarella

JCVD

Makes 8 open-faced sandwiches

Some people will tell you that you shouldn't put cheese on fish. Those people are living with weird rules for which nobody seems to even know the origins. Seriously, I just googled "Why can't I pair cheese with fish?" and the closest thing resembling an answer is "because Italians will get pissed off." I grew up with very little cultural identity. My mother's family is from the Midwest, via Utah, via Scotland, and nobody really seems to have cared a ton about food. And my dad was born in a part of Hungary that is now Romania, and perhaps because he didn't want to dwell too much on how much of his heritage the Nazis destroyed, or because he loves America with such fervor, he's never had much interest in instilling traditional Eastern European culture in me beyond chicken soup, fermented things, and sausages. He prefers hamburgers and barbecue. But as a chef, I am extremely thankful that I'm not constrained by the arbitrary rules of the past. Don't get me wrong; I think traditions are great and I hope that there are plenty of chefs who want to carry them on, but I, for one, like beans in my chili, flour in my corn tortilla dough, and for the sake of Jesus Christ himself, I love a tuna melt more than just about anything (I know, the tuna again!). So please don't read this recipe and spit on the floor, because that is gross. This sandwich is the most fucked-up English muffin pizza you've ever had and I guarantee that my late Hungarian grandpa Joe, who was one badass Jew (who by the way was in a little thing called World War I (on the side of an empire that no longer even exists!)) would love this sandwich, and that makes me happy.

- 2 cups Brussels sprouts, quartered if they're larger than your big toe, halved if they're smaller
- Kosher salt
- 1 tablespoon olive oil
- 1½ pounds mussels (I like the big bouchot mussels, but any mussels will be fine) cleaned and beards removed*
- 1 cup Old Bay Curry Sauce (PAGE 165)
- 4 English muffins, split in two with a fork like they are meant to be split
- 8 slices fresh mozzarella

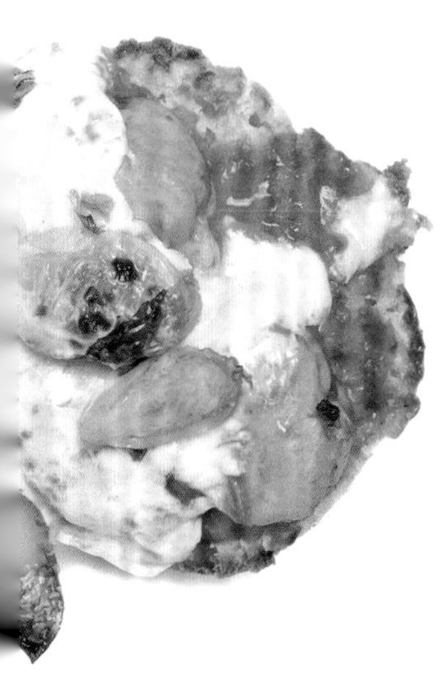

Preheat the oven to 450°F.

In a medium saucepan, combine the Brussels sprouts, 1 cup of water, and 1 teaspoon of salt. Bring to a boil over high heat and cook, uncovered, stirring a little at first and a lot at the end, until most of the water is evaporated. Transfer the Brussels sprouts to a bowl and toss with the olive oil.

Without cleaning the pot, add the mussels and curry sauce, cover, and cook on high until the mussels open, 3 to 5 minutes.

Pour the mussels and sauce into a colander set over a big bowl so that you can save the sauce. Let the mussels cool enough to touch them. Once they have cooled down, pull the mussels from the shells without being tempted by the fruit of your labor and eating them all. You can eat a couple of them, but be cool and remember the bigger picture.

Let's put these little beasts together. Lay out the English muffins on a baking sheet. Spoon a little of the mussels' sauce over each, and divide the mussels among them. Top each with a slice of mozzarella and finally some Brussels sprouts.

Put the sandwiches in the oven and cook until the muffins get nice and toasty and the Brussels sprouts get some color. If this is taking more than 5 to 8 minutes, then crank your oven all the way up and broil the little dudes for a minute to get some color on top. These are super hot now, so eat them slowly please. And you can eat two like *Double Impact*!

* Give the mussels a good rinse, and if they are super gnarly and barnacled on the outside, give them a scrub. Don't go crazy, because it's not like this step is going to make any difference in terms of food safety, and we're not serving them in the shells. You just want to make sure there's nothing gross hanging on there. If there are scruffy or hairy things hanging out of them (called, appropriately, beards), grab them and yank them out. And if any of your mussels don't close while you're doing all of this, then throw them away and give a very brief speech for each one of them. I never said this was going to be easy.

Ceviche • Hummus • Jicama Salad • Leche de Tigre Mayo

MI CORAZÓN LLORA

Makes 4 inauthentic sandwiches

Let's talk a little about authenticity. Ceviche is a dish from Peru, and people get upset when you mess with a dish from Peru. And so if you want to eat a dish from Peru, you should probably go to Peru or find a restaurant where they have a Peruvian chef. But if you want to see what happens when a chef from New York takes the idea of a tuna salad sandwich to a crazy place, then you should go to No. 7 Sub, because we think authenticity is in the eye of the beholder.

People love to yell, "That's not *authentic*!" and hammer you for it. But if a food is good, and it becomes popular and other people copy it, and it becomes commonplace on menus, then won't it be "authentic" in ten or twenty years? If we decide what is authentic today, and nothing that is created after today can be authentic, then what will people talk about in the future when they discuss 2015? In science, people are constantly building on what came before, but we're not supposed to do that in food? The equivalent would be that we stop using our iPhones because pay phones are authentic. I happen to like pay phones, and I guess I would be comfortable going back there. Also I have a lot of quarters in a jar, so I'm not hurting. You?

4 potato rolls

¼ cup Black Bean Hummus (PAGE 163)

¼ cup Leche de Tigre Mayo (PAGE 167)

2 cups drained Ceviche (PAGE 97)

½ cup Jicama Salad (PAGE 181)

8 sprigs cilantro leaves

¼ bunch scallions, chopped

1 lime, quartered

On the bottom buns put some hummus, and on the top put some of the mayo. Lay down some ceviche on top of the hummus, and please don't be shy on my account.

Top the ceviche with some jicama salad, cilantro, and scallions. Put the top bun on each sandwich and serve with a lime wedge on the side for squeezing. Limes on the side for squeezing are one of the true signs of adulthood. The others are good credit, not living with roommates, telling your parents that you smoke cigarettes, drinking a lot, smoking weed because you can and not because you are rebelling against someone, and sleeping six hours a night (because more sleep means that you're not doing enough or you are European).

VEGETABLE PUREES

Zucchini Parm

Fried Zucchini, Fontina, Onion Puree, Pickled Jalapeños, BBQ Potato Chips

•

Positive Mental Attitude

Crisped Pepperoni, Pickled Mushrooms, Granny Smith Apple, Yellow Squash Sauce

•

Gentle Thoughts

Asparagus, Carrot Puree, Shallot-Ginger Vinaigrette, Feta Cheese

•

Taken 2

Broccoli Falafel, Fennel Puree, Muchim Pickles, Tomatoes

FROM TOP TO BOTTOM:

Yellow squash puree, carrot puree, onion puree

BASIC VEGETABLE PUREE

Makes about 2 cups

Vegetable purees make a great base or sauce for sandwiches, or for eating with some meat, pasta, or other vegetables, even though that seems a little redundant. They add excellent flavor and a creamy texture without all the fat of a mayonnaise. This recipe will give you a concentrated punch of whatever vegetable you use. But you could definitely add other flavors like garlic, cumin, or coriander to take it in a different direction. And if you have half an onion, a couple of little chunks of butternut squash, and a turnip, feel free to combine them all into something amazing. Nobody can stop you from making the sandwich you want to make.

2 tablespoons olive oil or butter

1 pound Vidalia onion, carrot, or yellow squash (or pretty much any other vegetable), peeled and cut into ½-inch pieces

Kosher salt

Heat the oil in a medium saucepan over medium-low heat. Add your chosen vegetable and 1 teaspoon of salt and cook, stirring occasionally, until the vegetable is cooked but not caramelized. If it looks like it's going to start caramelizing, turn the heat down or splash in a little water. The carrot in particular will need a little water during the cooking process.

Once the vegetables are completely tender and the water is cooked off (the onion should take about 15 minutes, the squash about 10, and the carrot more like 20), transfer them to a blender.

If you have a fancy Vitamix, you can just attack and puree, using the plunger to keep things moving. But if you have a regular blender the veggies will be too thick and the blade of your blender will simultaneously "frappé" a little bit of veggie and push everything else away. The easy solution is to add just enough water so that the puree is unimpressed by the blender's coy reaction. The only problem with this is your puree will be a little runnier on your sandwich. There are worse problems in the world, so if this is a big one for you, maybe just ask your private chef to make you dinner? The other option is to puree, then stop the blender and use a rubber spatula to push the veggies back down into the blender. Turn the blender on again and repeat. This will take a little while, but you will get a thick and creamy puree that will make soccer more interesting. I'm just kidding. Nothing can make soccer more interesting.

Season the puree to taste with salt, and cool it down by placing it in a bowl set in another bowl of ice water.

Fried Zucchini • Fontina • Onion Puree • Pickled Jalapeños • BBQ Potato Chips

ZUCCHINI PARM

Makes 4 sandwiches or makes 1 hot sandwich and 3 of the best cold sandwiches. Seriously, this sandwich after a day in the fridge is like the world's greatest cold pizza.

This is one of the most popular sandwiches at No. 7 Sub. It's stayed on the menu longer than any other sandwich, and it will probably remain on the menu forever. It's just an eggplant parm, but I swapped out all of the ingredients. So it has fried zucchini instead of fried eggplant, fontina cheese instead of mozzarella, a sweet onion puree instead of tomato sauce, pickled jalapeños (because the acidity of the pickle makes up for the lack of acidity in the onion puree), and BBQ potato chips just because I wanted them. Did I mention that the Zucchini Parm is one of *my* all-time favorite sandwiches? I know this isn't very humble, but it's just one of those things that, while you know it's going to be good because you traded out the ingredients of something classic, and theoretically it's sound, it actually ends up transcending the original and making the angels in heaven punch each other in the mouth. That's when you know that you've done something right.

4 sub rolls, split lengthwise

½ cup onion puree (see PAGE 111)

1½ pounds Fried Zucchini (PAGE 150)

½ pound fontina cheese, sliced thin

½ cup Pickled Jalapeños (PAGE 177)

2 cups BBQ potato chips (see PAGE 183, or buy some)

Preheat the broiler.

On a baking sheet, arrange all of the bread halves cut side up. Put a tablespoon of onion puree on each piece.

On the bottom piece of each loaf, lay down some zucchini. Go big, because it's zucchini and it's cheap.

Can we talk for a second about "cheap"? Everybody thinks that an $11.75 sandwich is expensive. That's what we charge, and we don't make any money. And do you know why? It's because if you use real ingredients and pay somebody a reasonable wage to make sandwiches, you will not make any money. Everybody likes to talk about how you can still go to that place on the corner and get a $3 sandwich. And the truth is that you can, but their ingredients are garbage, and growing and shipping them is destroying the Earth, and the dude that is making your sandwich is making $6 an hour.

Enjoy that fucking $3 sandwich. I am content to be broke and do something awesome. At some point I will have to charge $15 for a sandwich. And we will go out of business, and I accept that. But at least I will sleep well at night. But back to zucchini!

Lay some fontina on that zucchini. Put both sides of all of the sandwiches under the broiler, meaning the fully loaded bottom, as well as the top that only has sauce on it. Cook it until the cheese is all melty and rad.

Pull everything out of the oven and top the cheesy zucchini side with pickled jalapeños and BBQ potato chips. Put the tops on and serve, while wondering if the food we buy and eat is expensive enough. I get it, you can't spend all of your money on food or it will make your life more difficult. But if you're not spending *enough* money on food, then you are making somebody else's life more difficult. Now I'm super bummed out, and I think I may have ruined one of my favorite sandwiches with the reality of the restaurant industry.

Crisped Pepperoni • Pickled Mushrooms • Granny Smith Apple • Yellow Squash Sauce

POSITIVE MENTAL ATTITUDE

Makes 4 sandwiches that would be banned in D.C.

Okay, I'm back. I'm calming down. But the next time I hear somebody say that something—anything—is overpriced, I am going to lose my mind and start screaming at them. Unless it's on Facebook and then I'll just leave the matter alone because I'm not crazy enough to argue with people on social media. [#SocialMedia #Hashtags #Crazy –#Ed.] #PMA

8 ounces pepperoni, sliced thin

4 potato rolls

½ cup yellow squash puree (see PAGE 111)

1 cup Pickled Mushrooms (PAGE 174)

½ Granny Smith apple

Lay the pepperoni slices out in a nonstick pan as you would bacon. Cook on medium heat for 6 to 8 minutes or so, until the pepperoni has rendered its fat and is crispy and brown on the edges. Drain on paper towels and save the pepperoni fat for later (scrambled eggs, roasted potatoes, etc.). In other words, we just treated pepperoni like bacon, and now we're looking at it and wondering why on Earth we've never done that before. We should do this all of the time! [Brilliant! This alone is probably worth the 20 bucks for the book. Or $11 if you bought it on Amazon and decided to put some poor small bookstore out of business. But I guess you could go to No. 7 Sub with the 9 bucks you have left over and have a sandwich.–Ed.]

Open the potato rolls and spoon the squash puree onto each side. Top with pepperoni and the mushrooms.

Using a Japanese mandoline with the medium-size teeth in place, cut the apple into a julienne. Or julienne the apple however you want. Honestly, whatever works. I can't even see how you do it, unless you post it to social media. Divide the apple between the 4 sandwiches. And I'm sorry that there is pepperoni on a sandwich that references Bad Brains, because I think they are all vegetarians, but I guess you could get vegetarian pepperoni.

Asparagus • Carrot Puree • Shallot-Ginger Vinaigrette • Feta Cheese

GENTLE THOUGHTS

Make 4 sandwiches

Just think about it: Would you rather buy a cheap car or an expensive hybrid car? I get it, you can't afford the hybrid, but you need a car so you buy the cheap one. But you get what you pay for, and your cheap car is contributing to wars in the Middle East and fracking in somebody's backyard, and in the long run it will cost you more because the hybrid you didn't buy barely needs gas. The same is true of your cheap food. It's contributing to environmental destruction, worldwide health concerns, and actual slavery. Not "These people are treated *like* slaves," but "These people are *actual* slaves." You can read about it in a book called *Tomatoland*, by Barry Estabrook. Or just read the reviews of it for free. I know that we can do better than that.

- 8 slices of cheap pumpernickel bread
- 1 bunch roasted asparagus (PAGE 56) or grilled asparagus (PAGE 57)
- ¼ cup Shallot-Ginger Vinaigrette (PAGE 166)
- ½ cup crumbled feta cheese
- ¼ cup carrot puree (see PAGE 111)

Lay out 4 slices of pumpernickel. Top each with asparagus, a tablespoon of vinaigrette, and some feta cheese.

Spread a spoonful of carrot puree on each of the remaining pieces of pumpernickel and close the sandwiches. And yes, I totally left the asparagus whole for the picture because it looks rad and I do want this upsetting book to also be pretty.

* We forgot the sesame seeds! This book is so upsetting!!!

Broccoli Falafel • Fennel Puree • Muchim Pickles • Tomatoes

TAKEN 2

Makes 4 "actually good" sandwiches

Sometimes people eat a vegan sandwich and say things like, "This is *actually* good!" and it makes all of the animals in the world cry. All food is good! If there is a large group of people who agree that a food tastes good, then chances are you will think it tastes good too! I think that people are way too focused on what vegan and vegetarian food is missing, as opposed to what it simply *is*. This sandwich is not vegan because I took things out to make it that way, even though it would be better with a bunch of meat and dairy on it. This sandwich is just this sandwich, and this sandwich happens to be vegan. And as I write that, I suddenly want this to be a whole book of vegetarian sandwiches, but I'm not going to go back through and take out all of the nonvegetarian things from these sandwiches, because then I would be a hypocrite and nobody likes that. But maybe if anybody buys this book and they let me write another one it will be called "A Super Upsetting Cookbook About Food That Happens to Be Vegetarian, but Had Nothing Removed to Make It That Way." [The contract is boilerplate, so we can draft it up any time. —Ed.]

4 hot dog buns

12 balls of Broccoli Falafel (PAGE 156)

½ cup onion puree (see PAGE 111)

¼ cup roughly chopped Cucumber Muchim (PAGE 69)

½ tomato, roughly chopped

1 tablespoon black sesame seeds

Open the hot dog buns and place 3 falafel into each one. Top with the onion puree, muchim, tomato, and sesame seeds. You also could put this sandwich inside of a pita, but then you also could have paid more attention in school and become a lawyer, but the relationship between high school and future success isn't super clear when you're sixteen, just like the relationship between certain breads and certain fillings eludes me even today. Kind of like how some people think that certain pasta shapes are better for certain sauces. I want everybody who has ever said "The ridges really hold on to the sauce" to take a step back and really think hard about whether we need to hear that from you anymore.

MEATLOAF

(His Name Is) Robert Paulson

Turkey Meatloaf, Shredded Cabbage Salad,
Marinara Sauce, Cilantro

•

Hot Patootie

Cold Meatloaf, Tomato Muchim,
Bacon Mayo, Bibb Lettuce

•

It Must Have Been While You Were Kissing Meatloaf

Meatloaf, Fennel Puree, Fresh Mozzarella,
Shrimp Muchim, Fried Shallots, Basil

•

This Article Is About Meatloaf. For the Singer, See Meat Loaf.

Meatloaf, Pho Mayo, Mint Jelly,
Pickled Bean Sprouts, Peanuts

Meatloaf is the answer!!! With meatloaf you can have your meat-cake and eat it too! Meatloaf is one of the best meat ideas ever created, because you can grind any cut of meat (meaning you're using up the less prized parts of an animal), you're stretching it further by adding vegetables and bread crumbs, and it's so delicious that you will think that you are British royalty while you eat it. I mean that in the sense that you will feel so lucky, like you are famous and rich for being born into the right family, which is the least difficult job of all of the jobs in the world. And how incredibly cool is the word *loaf*? Only certain things get to lay claim to fitting in with the word *loaf*. Bread, olive, meat—that's about the extent of nouns that apply to *loaf*. And the verb is just as cool! "I think I'll just loaf about and be a prince today." I say stuff like that all of the time.

But I Won't
Do That...

BASIC MEATLOAF

Makes about 2½ pounds, enough for 6 to 8 sandwiches

- **1 garlic clove (Sometimes restraint is more powerful than using a lot of garlic.)**
- **½ yellow onion, roughly chopped**
- **½ small carrot, roughly chopped**
- **1 broccoli stem***
- **2 pounds ground turkey, beef, lamb, veal, pork, elk, buffalo, ostrich, or a mix of some or all of them**
- **1 cup chopped bread, crust on, toasted if it isn't super stale**
- **1 egg**
- **2 teaspoons kosher salt**
- **2 teaspoons sugar**
- **¼ teaspoon ground mace**
- **½ teaspoon ground black pepper**
- **½ teaspoon ground coriander**
- **1 tablespoon white vinegar**
- **2 tablespoons sriracha sauce**
- **2 tablespoons grape jelly**
- **½ cup ketchup**

Preheat the oven to 300°F.

Put the garlic, onion, carrot, and broccoli stem (or whichever vegetable you need to use up) in a food processor and process until well chopped.

Put your glorious mush in a large mixing bowl with the meat, chopped bread, egg, salt, sugar, mace, black pepper, coriander, and white vinegar.

Using your bare hands, mix the ingredients together like your life depends on it. Because what if it actually does depend on it?!?!

In a roasting pan, shape the mixture into an awesome loaf, unless you don't trust me (which is pretty understandable), in which case you could make a small patty, sauté it in a pan, and taste it for seasoning. If you know what kind of sandwich you're going to make out of it, feel free to shape the loaf in such a way that its slices will fit your bread perfectly (though make it a little bigger than the bread because it will shrink when it cooks). Or, if you don't know what sandwich you'll make or even if you want it to go in a sandwich, then you should shape it like a *Tyrannosaurus rex* or your own initials or something fun like that.

In a small mixing bowl, whisk together the sriracha, grape jelly, and ketchup until smooth (or as smooth as you can get it, but some grape jelly likes to stay lumpy and it doesn't matter because it will melt when it cooks). Pour the glaze evenly over the loaf like you're frosting a cake with a spicy ketchup-based sauce.

Put the loaf in the oven and cook it for an hour to an hour and 15 minutes. It will be perfect. Don't overthink this. Or do, and use a thermometer to judge when it gets to an internal temperature of 150°F and it will be perfect, but at what cost? Are you actually satisfied with it? Are you ever satisfied with anything? Why did you buy this book when you still have so much to get through in *Modernist Cuisine*? That book looks like the end of the world; is that where you want to be? Throw away the thermometer and live your life!!

Let the meatloaf rest for 15 minutes and then slice it and destroy it with your mouth and your mind.

---

* Or small zucchini, small wedge of cabbage, half a bulb of fennel, 6 Brussels sprouts, or really any vegetable that you have in your fridge that you need to use up, roughly chopped (meatloaf is a little bit like making stock, meaning that it's like a delicious garbage disposal for meats and vegetables).

Turkey Meatloaf • Shredded Cabbage Salad • Marinara Sauce • Cilantro

(HIS NAME IS) ROBERT PAULSON

Makes 4 sandwiches that, like a bat out of hell, will be gone when the morning comes

Turkey meatloaf is the Gaby Hoffmann of meats. It was all over the place in the late '80s and early '90s, and then it disappeared. But turkey meatloaf and Gaby Hoffmann are back, and they're as amazing as ever!!

- 4 sub rolls
- 1 cup Marinara Sauce (PAGE 166)
- 4 big slabs of turkey meatloaf*
- 2 cups Shredded Cabbage Salad (PAGE 180)
- ½ cup fresh cilantro leaves

Split the sub rolls lengthwise because that just seems like the obvious way to cut them. Otherwise your bread-to-filling ratio is going to be super off, and the sandwich will look like Saturn.

Put some marinara sauce on either side of each half of bread. Put a slab of turkey loaf on each of the bottoms. Top with cabbage and cilantro.

* That's the meatloaf on page 124 but made with turkey and no other meats, though you can use any meat that you want. This is just the way we serve it at the sub shop.

Cold Meatloaf • Tomato Muchim • Bacon Mayo • Bibb Lettuce

HOT PATOOTIE

Makes 4 sandwiches

I was about to start this intro by talking about how much I like cold meatloaf. But the truth is I really like all food either cold or room temperature. I prefer my soup hot, but that's about it. Of course, I eat hot food all of the time, but only because sometimes I'm too hungry to wait for my food to cool down to room temperature. I wish there was a restaurant where they cooked things and then let them cool down and then served them to me. And I wish that it was called Dr. Doctor, because I always thought that was a really sweet name for a restaurant. "Dr. Doctor's Room Temperature Bar & Grill, serving the very best food that's been sitting around for a while."

- 4 slices preservative-riddled white bread
- ½ cup Bacon Mayo (PAGE 167)
- 4 slices of cold Meatloaf (PAGE 124; if you made it in the shape of a Mickey Mouse head, then I will have an ear, please)
- 8 slices Tomato Muchim (PAGE 69)
- 8 leaves Bibb lettuce

Lay out 4 slices of bread. Spread some mayo on each of them. Top them with a piece of meatloaf, 2 slices of tomato muchim, and 2 leaves of lettuce.

Spread some more mayo on the top slices of bread and close the sandwiches because you can eat as much mayo as you want. Don't cut these sandwiches in half because you don't have to, even if somebody says you have to. Somebody told me that I had to and so, to show them that I live my own life on my terms, I cut it into quarters and put pink swords in them.

Meatloaf • Fennel Puree • Fresh Mozzarella • Shrimp Muchim • Fried Shallots • Basil

IT MUST HAVE BEEN WHILE YOU WERE KISSING MEATLOAF

Makes 4 enormous meatball subs

The Meatloaf recipe on page 124 also works for making meatballs! But for a sandwich, you can just cook meatloaf and cover it with tomato sauce and call it a meatball sandwich. It's much easier to melt cheese on the flat slab, and it's easier to pile other things on top of it. Also, keeping it as a slab is a much more effective way to achieve the flavor of browned meat than making round balls and sautéing or roasting them to death trying to get an even crust. To me those meatballs always end up being chewy, and I am ambivalent about the crust anyway, so I prefer to poach my meatballs in the sauce itself.

Anyway, if you would prefer to roll this recipe into balls, stubbornly act like I am an asshole and prove that you make awesome meatballs by overcooking them in an attempt to make them a different color on the outside, be my guest! You probably know much more about Italian food than I do. Remember what I said on page 119 about pasta shapes? I am an idiot!

4 sub rolls, split lengthwise

1 cup fennel puree (see PAGE 111)

4 slabs of Meatloaf (PAGE 124; I vote pork meat loaf so that you can get that pork and shrimp combo going)

12 ¼-inch slices of fresh mozzarella

1 cup drained Shrimp Muchim (PAGE 69)

½ cup Fried Shallots (PAGE 175)

¼ cup basil leaves

Preheat the broiler.

Lay all of the rolls on a baking sheet, cut side up. Top each of the bottoms with 1 tablespoon of fennel puree, 1 slab of meatloaf, and 1 more tablespoon of fennel puree. On each of the tops, spread 1 tablespoon of fennel puree and 3 slices of mozzarella. Put the baking sheet under the broiler and cook, rotating the sandwiches to achieve even results, until all of the cheese is melted and a little caramelized and the fennel puree is bubbly and caramelized as well. Remove from the broiler and top each sandwich with some shrimp muchim, fried shallots, and basil leaves.

Meatloaf • Pho Mayo • Mint Jelly • Pickled Bean Sprouts • Peanuts

THIS ARTICLE IS ABOUT MEATLOAF. FOR THE SINGER, SEE MEAT LOAF.

Makes 4 sandwiches that are perfect for a picnic!

I think that if I ever get to write another cookbook, I would like to travel the world, making family meals at different restaurants and documenting it with photos and recipes. Maybe I would steal expensive ingredients from the first restaurant and cook them at the second. And then steal expensive ingredients from there and use them at the next one, and so on. Or maybe I would like to do a kind of science fiction/fantasy cookbook where I invent another world and its various cuisines and get super in-depth about regional differences in ingredients and techniques. Basically like *The Lord of the Rings*, only as a cookbook. And so here is the national sandwich of Vietkordistan. [The Pho Mayo is literally amazing. Tyler, imagine how many copies of this book we could have sold if it was just called "Mayo That Tastes like Pho, and Some Other Recipes." —Ed.]

8 slices white bread

¼ cup Pho Mayo (PAGE 168)

4 slabs of Meatloaf (PAGE 124)

1 tablespoon mint jelly

½ cup drained Pickled Bean Sprouts (PAGE 181)

¼ cup crushed peanuts

Lay out your sliced bread and spread some mayo on one side of each slice.

Top with the meatloaf, a drizzle of mint jelly, some pickled bean sprouts, and the crushed peanuts. This is kind of like a banh mi, but the pho mayo takes it to the next level of Vietnamese inspiration! It's kind of like catching all of the fat dripping off a chunk of barbecue brisket and using it to make hollandaise to put on your brisket eggs Benedict. This is next-level cooking. (Really Francis, you're just going to let that ride? "Next level"? What is this, Flavor Town?)

VEGGIE BURGERS

How Soon Is Now

Veggie Burger, Velveeta, Cucumber Muchim, Lettuce, Tomato, Bacon Mayo

•

Patty Melt!

Veggie Burger, Roasted Onions, Cheese

•

Gold Hat

Veggie Burger, No. 7 Steak Sauce, Red Onion, Fried Egg

•

Sympathy for the Devil

Veggie Burger, Avocado Blue Cheese, Roasted Onions

There are a lot of different kinds of veggie burgers out there. They can generally be put into three main categories.

Beany/Grainy: This kind of veggie burger—grains or veggies held together by beans—can be super delicious but often ends up being mushy and smooshing out the sides of the bun. I do not hate this kind of veggie burger, but I also do not need for it to exist in my life. I mean, we already have falafel! And falafel is its own real thing, and it's too proud to pretend to be a fake version of something else. Falafel. So strong.

Fake Meaty: This veggie burger seems like it's trying to attract vegetarians who are vegetarian for ethical or health reasons but who would prefer to keep eating meat. It tends to be dense and chewy and made of soy products or seitan. I got really into these in high school. With all of the usual condiments (ketchup, mayo, pickles, lettuce, tomato, etc.), they taste a lot like McDonald's hamburgers, which are both excellent and the end of the world.

Super Vegetabley: These are made from a bunch of loosely bound chopped vegetables (peas, corn, etc.). This kind of veggie burger tends to be fairly crumbly, tastes nothing like a hamburger, and is totally unapologetic about that. Of the three, this one tends to be my favorite. This veggie burger is to the burger lexicon what Michel Gondry is to film.

The veggie burger produced by this recipe is a hybrid of the last two categories. We will grind seitan (a move I learned from my good friend Elena Balletta) and mix it with roasted and shredded broccoli for a lighter, more vegetal flavor. It's a little crumbly, but it's similar to the way ground meat crumbles, and it doesn't taste like a burger, but it does taste like something totally awesome, and that is fun. And my buddy Jeff and I figured out how to make it vegan!! And this is the easiest veggie burger recipe of all time! You can throw this together and get your kids to eat their veggies in no time. [Wu-Tang is for the babies! This book is for the babies! —Ed.]

Veggie Burger • Velveeta • Cucumber Muchim • Lettuce • Tomato • Bacon Mayo

HOW SOON IS NOW

Makes 4 burgers that shred your brains

I know that I said that I don't like cheese and bacon on burgers, and this burger appears to have cheese and bacon on it. But the Bacon Mayo doesn't actually have bacon in it, Velveeta is not actually cheese, and veggie burgers have different rules than beef burgers because I said so.

- 4 Veggie Burgers (PAGE 136)
- 4 chunks/slices Velveeta (or whatever cheese you like, but Velveeta is weird and delicious!)
- 4 hamburger buns
- 1 tablespoon melted unsalted butter or olive oil (optional)
- ¼ cup Bacon Mayo (PAGE 167)
- 12 Cucumber Muchim chips (PAGE 69)
- 4 pieces of your favorite lettuce
- 4 to 8 slices of beefsteak tomato, depending on how much tomato you like on your burgers

Heat the oven to 400°F.

Place the veggie burgers on a baking sheet and top each one with some Velveeta. Put them in the oven to cook until the cheese is melted, about 3 minutes.

While the burgers are in the oven, brush the buns with the butter or olive oil, and toast them in the oven too. You can skip this step if you'd like, because for me nothing is better than a fresh, untoasted hamburger bun. But our burgers are in the oven, and if we don't toast the bun we'll just make another drink.

Transfer the buns to plates and put a little bit of bacon mayo on each one. Top each of the bottoms with a veggie burger and pile on the muchim, lettuce, and tomato. Do not cut this burger in half. For some reason it really drives me crazy when people cut burgers in half. I think it's because your burger halves are now taller than they are wide, and that's just stupid. And you don't cut a slice of pizza in half to make it easier to eat, so why should a burger not get the same respect?

BASIC VEGGIE BURGERS

Makes 6 burgers (Yes, I know all the sandwich recipes call for 4 burgers but when was the last time you were sad there were extra burgers?)

2 tablespoons cornstarch

1½ cups of ½-inch chunks of seitan

1 cup chopped roasted broccoli (PAGE 56)

6 tablespoons dry bread crumbs

1 teaspoon kosher salt

Vegetable oil, for cooking

In a small mixing bowl, combine the cornstarch with 2 tablespoons of water and mix with a fork until the cornstarch is completely dissolved.

In a food processor, combine the cornstarch slurry, seitan, broccoli, bread crumbs, and salt, and process until there are no more big chunks and everything is thoroughly mixed. It will look like a strange green oatmeal. Transfer to a bowl and let rest in the refrigerator for at least 30 minutes and up to four days covered.

When you are ready for burgers, divide the burger mixture into sixths, shape the portions into rough balls by rolling them in your hands, and gently press them into patties. I like to use a ring mold to make prettier patties, but you probably don't have one of those, and I applaud your rustic sensibility.

Heat a large sauté pan over medium heat with enough oil to slick the pan. When the oil shimmers, place as many patties as will fit comfortably in the pan. Once you see the edges start to caramelize, after about 3 minutes, carefully flip the patties and cook an additional 2 minutes. Put the burgers on buns with whatever toppings make you feel badass, listen to "The Boys Are Back in Town" by Thin Lizzy, eat your super-awesome veggie burger, and flip people off from the window.

Veggie Burger • Roasted Onions • Cheese

PATTY MELT!

Makes 4 seriously outrageous patty melts

What's fun about making and trying out new veggie burgers is that there is no real notion of what a veggie burger should be. There are veggie burgers out there, and they range from terrible to incredible, just like any food, but we haven't found the ceiling yet. It's not like with pizza, where, over the past several hundred years, we have determined the best ingredients for making it, and we have figured out the exact best one or two ways to cook it. We know what it tastes like in its perfect form. Veggie burgers are a relatively new phenomenon, and we're still trying to figure out what they taste like, and how fun is that? What if this book is to the real future as Wyld Stallyns music is to the future in *Bill and Ted's Excellent Adventure*? What if this *is* the perfect veggie burger?!?

- 4 Veggie Burgers (PAGE 136)
- 4 tablespoons (½ stick) salted butter (I know! (but remember how much more fat you would be consuming if you made this with ground beef!))
- 8 slices rye bread (not that bullshit rye bread without caraway seeds)
- 8 to 12 slices of cheese (I like a lot of cheese. Maybe Cheddar?)
- 1 cup Roasted Onions (see PAGE 172)

After cooking your veggie burgers, remove them to a plate, add 2 tablespoons of the butter to the pan, and melt it over medium heat. Place 4 slices of rye bread in the pan and top each one with one-eighth of the cheese, a veggie burger, one-fourth of the onions, another eighth of the cheese, and another slice of rye bread. Press the sandwiches down a little and cook until they are nicely browned and crispy on the bottom, 6 to 8 minutes. Carefully flip them, add the remaining 2 tablespoons of butter to the pan, and cook, occasionally moving them around to make sure the butter is evenly distributed, until that side is also browned, 6 to 8 minutes.

Serve with pickles and a sauce, such as Smoked French Dressing (page 162), for dipping.

Veggie Burger • No. 7 Steak Sauce • Red Onion • Fried Egg

GOLD HAT

Makes 4 sloppy burgers

A fried egg on a burger is so super delicious because an egg yolk is one of the best sauces of all time. But be advised, this sandwich is a mess! Maybe just quarter the recipe and only make enough for yourself (or cut it in half, because nobody is watching and you can eat two burgers if you want to eat two burgers!) and then eat it in your bedroom with only a reading lamp and *The Treasure of the Sierra Madre* to illuminate the sauce and egg yolk all over your shirt.

4 Veggie Burgers (PAGE 136)

4 hamburger buns, toasted or not, your choice

2 tablespoons No. 7 Steak Sauce (PAGE 167)

1 tablespoon unsalted butter

4 eggs

Kosher salt

¼ cup thinly sliced red onion

Cook your veggie burgers and put them on the bun bottoms. Top them with a little bit of steak sauce.

While that is happening, let's fry some eggs, shall we? I don't love a crust on my fried eggs, so I cook them relatively slowly in a nonstick pan. If you like the crust, or you don't have a nonstick pan, or you have an old nonstick pan that isn't really nonstick anymore, then you'll want to cook these over higher heat.

So, assuming you agree with me (and why wouldn't you agree with me? I am always right!), heat a large nonstick pan over medium heat. Add the butter, melt it, and reduce the heat to medium low. Crack your eggs into the pan and season them with salt. Cook, moving the eggs occasionally until the whites have cooked through and the yolks are cooked a little more than you would normally cook them for sunny-side-up eggs. Putting a fried egg on a sandwich is messy no matter what you do, but if you cook the egg a little more you'll have a thicker sauce that will stay on the sandwich a little better. Feel free to flip the egg or put a lid on the pan for a minute to achieve this, but know that if you overcook the top of your egg, it will be less beautiful and your friends will be less impressed. But it will still be delicious, so don't worry about what they think! And I thought we agreed that you were going to eat this alone anyway!

Put an egg on top of each burger and finish them with a little bit of red onion.

Veggie Burger • Avocado Blue Cheese • Roasted Onions

SYMPATHY FOR THE DEVIL

Makes 4 stinky but beautiful burgers

The first time I ever had blue cheese on a burger was at the Spotted Pig. It was so delicious that I almost exploded. You know how blue cheese can smell like feet sometimes? That's because the bacteria that makes blue cheese so stinky is the same one that causes body odor and stinky feet. Doesn't that make you want to die just a little since you just bought half a pound of soft cheese full of unclean-person bacteria? Don't think too much about it. This is a nice, simple burger that pairs perfectly with *Interview with the Vampire* and thinking about Tom Cruise.

4 hamburger buns

4 Veggie Burgers (PAGE 136)

½ cup Avocado Blue Cheese (PAGE 181)

½ cup Roasted Onions (PAGE 172)

Lay out your buns, cut side up. Place a cooked veggie burger on each one. Spread a tablespoon of avocado blue cheese onto each of the tops. Pile some of the roasted onions on top of each burger. Close the sandwich and eat it. You can totally eat two of these by yourself. Don't think, just do it!

MAIN (OR ALMOST-MAIN, BUT DON'T TELL THEM THAT) COMPONENTS

Fried Clams

Makes enough for 2 clam sandwiches or to garnish 4 to 6 sandwiches

I like clams more every day. They're funky and briny and delicious, and littlenecks from the East Coast are nice and sustainable, so nobody can get all huffy. Even after they've been steamed open, breaded, and fried, they're still nice and tender, and even if you overcook them slightly, a little chew ain't so bad in a sandwich. If you're hard core, you can skip the first step, shuck them raw, and get straight to the breading, but I don't think that's necessary. You could also get preshucked clams, but I just don't think that's a good idea. They taste weird. But I make bad decisions all of the time, so who am I to judge?

1 pound littleneck clams, rinsed and scrubbed thoroughly of sand

1 egg white

1½ tablespoons cornstarch

2 cups panko bread crumbs

Vegetable oil, as needed

Kosher salt

Put the clams in a pot with ¼ inch or so of water. Put a lid on the pot and cook on high heat, stirring occasionally until almost all the clams are open. Dump the clams into something big and metal. Pull out the unopened ones and cook them a little more in the hopes that they're just stubborn. If they still don't open after a few minutes, assume they are dead and bury them. (Don't eat them.) Cool the clams.

Combine the egg white and the cornstarch in a mixing bowl and whisk until smooth. When the clams are cool, shuck the meat out of the shells and discard the shells. Put the juice in the freezer for soup or Bloody Caesars.

Fill a large saucepan or small stockpot with 2 to 3 inches of oil, making sure the pot is a few inches taller than the level of the oil. Set it over medium heat until it reaches 400°F on a candy/frying thermometer. (If you don't have one of those, get one. Or look and see if the oil looks really weirdly wavy inside and a bread crumb sizzles instantly when you drop it in.)

While the oil is heating, put enough of the egg white/cornstarch goo to coat the clams in a mixing bowl. Add the clam meat and toss real good. Put the panko in a different bowl, lift the clams out of the egg whites, and put them on top of the panko. Toss the clams gently in the panko and make sure they are all separated.

When the clams and the oil are ready, increase the heat to medium high. Shake off any excess panko and fry the clams, a few at a time, just until golden brown, about 2 minutes. Remove them with a slotted spoon or strainer and drain on paper towels while you fry the next batch. Season the hot clams with a little salt (not too much because the clams come with their own salt!).

Garam Masala Corned Beef

Makes 3 to 4 pounds, enough for a lot of sandwiches, because what is the point of doing this if you're not going to make enough to last a while?

The spices used for corned beef and the spices used in lots of Indian curries are pretty much exactly the same, but in different proportions. Madhur Jaffrey has a super-neat book (*From Curries to Kebabs: Recipes from the Indian Spice Trail*) about how British imperialism carried curry all over the world; any of her books are perfect if you want to find a super-authentic recipe for garam masala. She doesn't really touch on corned beef, but being the son of a Hungarian/Romanian/Cleveland Jew and eating at Corky and Lenny's whenever possible, I think about corned beef a lot. And so I read her book and came up with this extremely inauthentic dish that basically tastes like really good corned beef, but just gets there in a weird way.

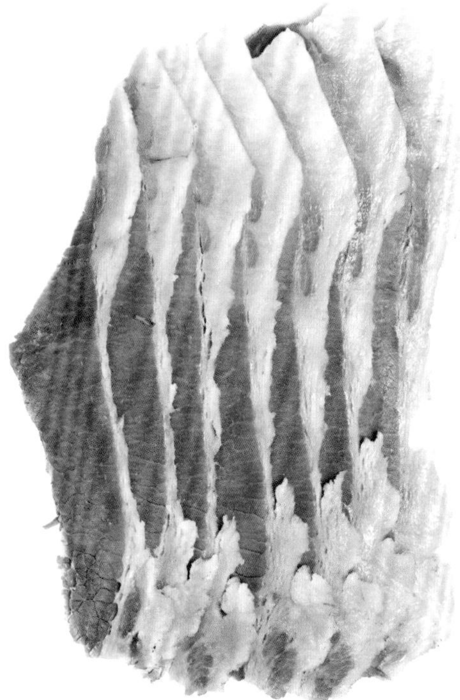

¾ cup salt

3 tablespoons sugar

1 tablespoon pink curing salt* (optional)

4 garlic cloves, roughly chopped

1 1-inch piece ginger, cut into ¼-inch slices

2 tablespoons garam masala, toasted (you can use the store-bought stuff or follow one of the millions of recipes on the Internet (why do you need this book when you have the Internet?))

3 to 4 pounds beef (the conventional wisdom is to use brisket, but I prefer short ribs)

* Pink curing salt is a mixture of sodium nitrite, table salt, and a little bit of red dye so that you don't accidentally season your eggs with it. It ensures that your meat is safe from bacteria while brining or curing it, but brining and curing were the original ways of making meat safe in the first place. A lot of people think that pink curing salt causes cancer because some rats died after being fed huge amounts of it. I don't really buy that. So maybe make your own choices here.

In a medium saucepan over medium heat, combine the salt, sugar, curing salt, garlic, ginger, and garam masala with 2 quarts of water. Bring just to a simmer, and then turn off the heat, stirring to make sure that everything gets dissolved. Cool the brine completely.

Put the beef and brine together in a plastic container. Place a small plate or something nonreactive on top of the beef to keep it submerged in the brine. Cover the container and keep it in the refrigerator for five days. Sit and think about the fact that you are working on a sandwich that you won't eat for at least five days and really question that.

Pull the beef out of the brine, discard the brine, and rinse off the beef with fresh water. Put it in a pot and add enough water to cover the beef. Turn the heat to high, bring to a boil, and reduce the heat to a gentle simmer, cooking for 2½ to 3 hours, or until the meat is tender. If you're cooking a relatively lean piece of meat, you don't want to go too long or it will get super dry, so I tend to err on the side of a tiny bit of extra chew but still super moist. Anyway, when it's tender, take the beef out of the pot and let it cool.

Canadian Bacon

Makes 4 to 5 pounds, which is a lot of Canadian bacon, so don't do this unless you're committed to a life full of surprises and happiness.

Canadian bacon, or back bacon, is bacon made from the loin of a pig, usually with a little bit of belly meat hanging on at one end. It is bacon's leaner cousin who comes to visit every once in a while and completely trashes your apartment, which is, I think, why you don't eat it as much as regular belly bacon.

1 cup maple syrup

¾ cup kosher salt

1 tablespoon pink curing salt (see * at left), optional

1 teaspoon ground allspice

1 tablespoon cracked black pepper

1 cup loose Lapsang souchong tea leaves

4 garlic cloves, roughly chopped

4 to 5 pounds boneless pork loin

1 tablespoon canola oil

In a medium pot, combine the maple syrup, salt, pink curing salt, allspice, pepper, tea, garlic, and 2 quarts of water. Bring just to a boil over high heat. Remove from the heat and cool completely.

Put the pork in a nonreactive container with high sides and completely cover the pork with brine. Put a couple plates on top of the pork to keep it submerged in the brine. Cover the container and put it in the fridge for five days.

After the five days are up, preheat the oven to 300°F.

Pull the pork out of the brine and rinse and dry it thoroughly. Put the pork in a roasting pan, rub it with the oil, and roast it in the oven until it is cooked all of the way through and its internal temperature is 140°F to 150°F. Cool the pork and keep it whole; slice and reheat when you want to eat it.

Fried Eggplant

Makes enough for 4 to 6 sandwiches

Listen, you can't eat fried broccoli all of the time. Sometimes you have to fry other things too! And when that need arises, look to your old friend eggplant. I think I am a tiny bit allergic to eggplant because when I eat it my tongue gets all tingly. But it hasn't killed me, and so it must be making me stronger. That's why I've stopped going to the gym, because I don't want to get too super strong. Nobody really likes people with muscles.

Vegetable oil, for frying

½ cup all-purpose flour

¼ cup cornstarch

1 tablespoon kosher salt

1 teaspoon sesame oil

2 teaspoons balsamic vinegar

1 teaspoon baking powder

1 cup panko bread crumbs

1 large eggplant, peeled and sliced into ½-inch rounds

Put 3 inches of oil in a large saucepan, making sure there are a couple inches of clearance, and heat it over medium heat to 375°F on a candy/frying thermometer. (If you don't have one of those, get one. Or look and see if the oil looks really weirdly wavy inside and a bread crumb sizzles instantly when you drop it in.)

Make the tempura batter: In a medium mixing bowl, whisk together the flour, cornstarch, salt, sesame oil, balsamic vinegar, baking powder, and ¾ cup of cold water until smooth.

Line a plate with paper towels because you don't want to be caught with your pants down after frying eggplant in 375°F oil.

Put all of the eggplant into the tempura batter and mix it around so that all of the eggplant is totally coated.

With a pair of tongs, pick up a piece of eggplant and let a little of the excess batter drain off. Drop it in the panko and toss to coat. Repeat that process with a couple more pieces of eggplant and, when the oil is ready, turn the heat up to medium high and fry the eggplant, a few slices at a time, for 1 minute. Flip them all and then let them fry for another minute. When they are golden and spectacular, remove them from the oil and let them drain on the paper towel–lined plate. Working in batches, repeat this process with the rest of the eggplant.

Chicken-Fried Mushrooms

Makes enough for 4 sandwiches

This recipe comes from my friend and one of my old bosses, Patrick Farrell. Patrick is from Fort Worth, Texas, can whistle any Beatles album from start to finish, taught me most of what I know about cooking, and makes the best fried chicken I have ever had in my life. The key ingredient to Patrick's fried chicken is restraint. There are very few ingredients; it's really just about proper seasoning and technique. (And hey, where are you guys buying your chickens from that you need to soak them in buttermilk to tenderize them? If you think chicken is tough then you must eat a lot of pudding.)

I can't give you Patrick's fried chicken recipe, because Patrick is protective of these things, but I will say that it is similar to this one. Patrick is in fact so protective of his two finest achievements, fried chicken and chili, that he never showed me how to make them, but I am sneaky and I watched closely every time, and now I am one of the very few

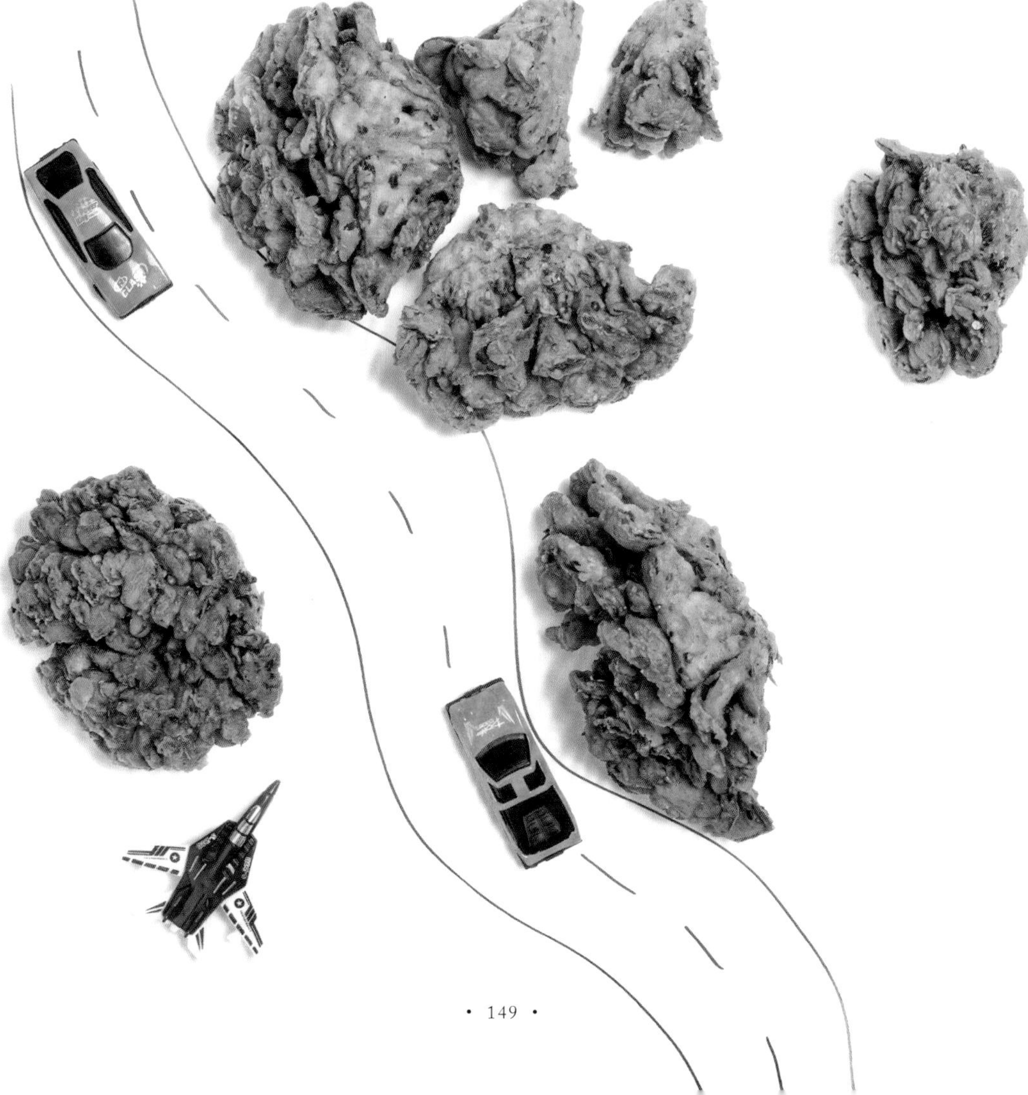

who holds the secrets. You can use this same frying technique for chicken, but know that it's a little different than Patrick's version. Anyway, this recipe is for mushrooms! I like maitakes because they look like brains, but you could use any mushrooms that are nice and big, such as porcinis, portobellos, or king oysters, or even some nice big button mushrooms. Or you can use small ones, but then it will take you a while to bread them all.

1 quart vegetable or canola oil, for frying

2 dried shiitake mushrooms

1 cup all-purpose flour

3 teaspoons kosher salt, plus more to taste

1 tablespoon ground black pepper

1 egg

1 cup whole milk

1 pound maitake (or other) mushrooms, cut into 4 portions

Heat the oil in a large saucepan or stockpot over medium heat to 350°F on a candy/frying thermometer. (If you don't have one of those, get one. Or look and see if the oil looks really kinda wavy inside and if you drop your phone in, it starts to melt just a little at the corners and you feel an overwhelming sense of relief. Also if a pinch of flour sizzles instantly in it.)

Using a spice grinder or blender, grind the dried shiitakes as fine as you can get them (that was my dear friend Jeffrey Maslanka's idea). In a medium mixing bowl, combine the flour, 2 teaspoons of the salt, the pepper, and the ground mushrooms. Mix thoroughly.

In a separate medium bowl, crack the egg and whisk it until the yolk and white are well mixed. Pour 3 tablespoons of it into another container and save it for someone you love. It is crucial that you get rid of most of that egg, as a whole egg is too much for breading. The protein will help the breading hold together, but it will also make it doughier. So finding the right amount of egg is important, and it turns out it isn't much. Add the milk and the remaining teaspoon of salt to the egg and whisk to combine.

Now do the move where you take a piece of mushroom and roll it in the seasoned flour, pat off the excess flour, roll it in the milk-egg mixture, and then put it back into the flour. Transfer it to a plate and repeat with the rest of the mushrooms.

Fry the mushrooms a few pieces at a time for 4 to 6 minutes, or until golden brown and amazing. Remove and drain on paper towels, and sprinkle some salt on the mushrooms while they're still hot.

Fried Zucchini

Makes enough for 4 sandwiches

You've had fried zucchini before, and you know that you like it. We're going to bread it using a super-excellent technique that I learned from Jean-Georges Vongerichten when I worked at Perry Street many years ago. It's this cornstarch/egg-white move that makes things so crispy that you may have to warn people so that they don't hurt themselves. That level of crispy is crucial for a sandwich because the sauces and such can make fried things disappear. A little soggy is fine, but you need some of the crunch to survive, or why did you bother frying in the first place?

Vegetable or canola oil, for frying

2 egg whites

3 tablespoons cornstarch

2 large zucchini or 4 small ones

2 cups panko bread crumbs

Kosher salt

In a large saucepan, heat 4 inches of the oil over medium heat to 400°F on a candy/frying thermometer. (If you don't have one of those, get one. Or look and see if the oil looks really weirdly wavy inside (#deepfat) and a bread crumb sizzles instantly when you drop it in.)

In a mixing bowl, whisk together the egg whites and cornstarch. Wash the zucchini and slice them on the bias into ½-inch-thick slices.

One piece at a time, dip the zucchini into the cornstarch/egg-white mixture and then hold it up out of the bowl to let excess batter drip off. Next drop it in the panko and roll it around. Be gentle! Remove the piece of breaded zucchini and put it on a tray. Repeat this process with all of the zucchini.

When the oil is ready, turn the heat up to medium high. Fry the zucchini, working in batches so that there's some space in between each piece, until it is deep golden brown. Drain on paper towels and season well with salt. Do not take a bite out of that zucchini or you will burn your stupid and impatient mouth! Wait a few minutes and then you can do it.

Fried Tofu

Makes enough for 4 sandwiches

I'm not super into tofu unless it's fried. I realize that frying things is unhealthy, so I don't recommend eating fried foods every day, but I also don't think you should eat meat every day, so if it takes frying things to get you to let the meat go, then I'm all for it.

A lot of people say you should press your tofu before frying because it gets the moisture out and it's firmer and more like, I dunno, chicken. With this technique you don't press it, and the resulting tofu has a crispy-on-the-outside, custardy-on-the-inside feel, which is a pretty awesome contrast. But I realize that you know better than me, so go ahead and press your tofu, because I obviously can't stop you, and it obviously makes you feel better to be right all of the time. I would hate to be right all of the time. I realize that the tone of this book may make me sound confident, but that's just because I am alone in a room with nobody to tell me I'm stupid, and no real sense of what a bummer it will be when this book comes out and everybody hates it, or even worse, nobody cares about it at all. I really wish you would stop pressing your tofu to make it more like chicken! If you don't like tofu, then why are you eating it anyway?!

1 quart canola or vegetable oil, for frying

1 pound firm tofu, drained and cut into 8 slices

Kosher salt

3 large egg whites

3 tablespoons cornstarch

1 cup panko bread crumbs

Heat the oil in a large saucepan over medium heat to 375°F on a candy/frying thermometer. (If you don't have one of those, then you are probably living and enjoying your life. Cheers! Or look and see if the oil looks really weirdly wavy inside and a bread crumb sizzles instantly when you drop it in.)

Season the tofu slices with just a tiny bit more salt than you feel comfortable with. Don't worry, the sodium won't kill you. That's probably a combination of a generally poor diet, lack of exercise, depression, excessive drinking, lying to people, narcissism, and sodium, and see—salt is the last thing on the list. Frankly, with modern medicine, you will probably live for another ten years after society has crumbled and everybody lives underground, eating insects and worshipping the last remaining canned goods. Do you really want to see that? Season that tofu with abandon.

In a small mixing bowl, combine the egg whites and cornstarch and whisk until the cornstarch is fully dissolved and the mixture is smooth.

Take a piece of tofu and completely coat it with the goo. Hold it up over the bowl of goo and let most of the excess drip off. Next place it into the panko bread crumbs and gently toss it around so that the panko coats the whole thing. Do not try to press the panko on there or it will just fall off and ridicule your ineffectiveness. I'm sorry, this is a super-mean recipe. Let's turn it around here.

Repeat with the remaining tofu until all of it is coated and breaded and smiling up at you and confirming that, yes, there is joy in the world, and it comes in the form of frying those little disapproving tofu cakes until they are crispy and delicious and nobody can hear their screams of terror. See what I just did there?

When the oil is ready, turn the heat up to medium high. Working in batches, fry the tofu until brown and crispy, about 5 minutes, flipping halfway to make sure both sides get brown and crispy. Drain on paper towels. If you're going to just eat it, then season the outside with a little salt. If you're going to coat it in a sauce, then no salt is necessary.

Soft-Boiled Fried Eggs

Makes 8 eggs

Make these all of the time. They're delicious, your friends will be impressed, and more importantly, if you bring someone home after a date and fry up some of these, you will not necessarily get laid, but if getting laid was already in the cards, and you and the person you might have sex with are hungry, then this will make sure that everybody has a good amount of fat, protein, and salt to really feel good about the situation.

8 eggs

Vegetable oil, for frying

3 large egg whites

½ cup cornstarch

1 cup panko bread crumbs

Kosher salt

Fill a large stockpot halfway with water and bring it to a boil over high heat. Set a timer for 7 minutes, but don't start it yet. When the water is boiling, very gently add the eggs, being careful not to drop them too hard or they will crack and they won't look as awesome, though they'll be just as delicious. Start the timer! When the timer goes off, cool the eggs in a bowl with some ice water.

In a large saucepan, heat 3 inches of the oil over medium heat to 400°F on a candy/frying thermometer. (If you don't have one of those, get one. Or look and see if the oil looks really weirdly wavy and a bread crumb sizzles instantly when you drop it in. Frying things at home is like living at McDonald's! Childhood you is winning!!)

Once the eggs are cooled, peel them, but be gentle because they're only soft-boiled and pretty delicate. We made 8 eggs so that you would end up with 6 or so nice ones, so it's not the end of the world if you break a couple. Let the eggs hang out and dry off on paper towels.

In a small mixing bowl, combine the egg whites and cornstarch and whisk until the cornstarch is fully dissolved and the mixture is smooth.

Dip an egg in the cornstarch/egg-white mixture and let the excess drain off. Gently toss it in the panko and then put it on a plate while you repeat the process with the rest of the eggs.

When the oil is ready, turn the heat up to medium high and fry the eggs in two batches, flipping occasionally, until golden brown, about 2 minutes. Drain on paper towels and immediately season well with salt.

Fried Fish

Makes enough fried fish for 4 huge sandwiches or 6 reasonable sandwiches

I think that if I were to hold a Tournament of Fried Food Champions inside of my own head, fried fish would not even break a sweat until it came up against my favorite fried thing of them all: french fries. Strangely, I am not a big fan of fish-and-chips because it's just a little more fried food than I really need to get involved with. But in a sandwich or a taco, or just on its own with some fun sauces for dipping, fried fish is a safe space for me. I prefer a white, flaky fish like pollock or hake. Unfortunately, my absolute favorite fish of all fish is Atlantic cod, which has huge, glorious flakes, but which is also so overfished that it is virtually endangered. But boycotting Atlantic cod is one of those complicated situations because there are a lot of people on the East Coast for whom cod fishing is their primary livelihood. I hope that somebody smarter than me figures out how to fix the cod system before they are all gone *and* everybody is out of work. It's easy to sit back and say that nobody should fish for cod anymore, but when you actually think about all of the jobs—not just fishing jobs, but everything from fixing boats to selling gas for the boats to driving trucks—that would just cease to exist if the cod industry goes away, it's just absolutely heartbreaking. But if the fish aren't there, then what can be done? Yes, there are literally plenty of fish in the sea, but I have a hard time selling tilefish (which is delicious!) in my restaurant in a neighborhood where people are supposedly a little bit knowledgeable about aquatic issues, so how are we supposed to suddenly have a tilefish industry? Again, it's more complicated than a simpleton like me can figure out, so maybe let's stick to haddock for this dish, but it's worth thinking about. Sorry to get all serious there.

Vegetable oil, for frying

1½ pounds fish, cut into long, thin fillets*

Kosher salt to taste

1½ cups rice flour

1 teaspoon baking soda

1 cup beer**

½ cup cornstarch

1½ cups all-purpose flour

* To put it in candy terms, we're talking Skor if you're using flounder or something else really thin, and 5th Avenue if your fish is a little thicker. At the end of the day, they can be as thick as you want, but if they're super thick, they will take forever to cook and stay so hot that they will burn your mouth the entire time that you're eating the sandwich. They will become cool enough to eat when you have exactly one bite left.

** Any beer that you like will work for this, and don't let anybody tell you otherwise. Those same people will only use certain pasta shapes with certain sauces. "Orecchiette is for meat sauces because I have nothing better to talk about. You're not going to make a beer batter with *Guinness*, are you?"

Heat 3 inches of oil in a large Dutch oven over medium heat to 375°F on a candy/frying thermometer. (If you don't have one of those, get one. Or look and see if the oil looks wavy inside and a bread crumb sizzles instantly when you drop it in.)

Season your fish all over with salt and put the fish aside for now.

In a small mixing bowl, combine the rice flour, baking soda, and 2 teaspoons of kosher salt and whisk until totally mixed. Add the beer and whisk until fairly smooth; you don't need to get it super smooth.

Put the cornstarch in a shallow bowl and the flour in a different shallow bowl.

Coat a piece of fish in the cornstarch and then put it in a colander over the sink. Repeat with all of the fish. Shake the colander a bunch until all the excess cornstarch has fallen off the fish fillets.

One at a time, dip a piece of fish in the batter, hold it up over the bowl so that some of the excess drips off, and then put it in the bowl with the flour and toss it around to coat it. Transfer the piece of fish to a plate and repeat with the rest of the fish.

When the oil is ready, turn the heat up to medium high. Working in batches so as not to reduce the oil temperature too much, fry the fish fillets, turning occasionally, until golden brown and awesome, 2 to 4 minutes, depending on how thick you cut them. Remove and let them drain on a paper towel–lined plate, and sprinkle them with salt while they're still hot.

Perfect Scrambled Eggs

Makes 4 scrambled eggs, about 1 cup

Scrambled eggs are one of the first things anybody ever learns to cook, and while there are many ways to do it and all of them are good, there is one perfect way, and that is what I'm about to describe to you. But be advised, there isn't much in the way of secrets here; you just have to be super in tune with your eggs and practice a few times, and then you will be a champion of this. I have successfully wooed women with scrambled eggs before. Okay, one time I made scrambled eggs for a woman who was already pretty into me, but I think the eggs, and their ability to make her forget about the fact that her friend was hammered and puking in the bathroom, are what really made her fall in love with me. In the end, I screwed that relationship up pretty bad, and no amount of eggs will ever convince her that I am not a terrible person, but it may not be too late for you!

4 eggs

1 teaspoon unsalted butter

½ teaspoon kosher salt

Crack the eggs into a blender and puree on the lowest setting until the eggs are totally uniform. This is the only "secret" to making scrambled eggs. I am too stupid to know why, but for some reason, when the whites and yolks are completely mixed together, your scrambled eggs will taste better than if they are only partially mixed with a fork. I think it's that the uniformity in protein composition allows the eggs to cook more evenly and gives you a much smoother texture or some other stupid thing like that. They are so delicious, people will ask if you put milk or cheese in them, and you will say, "No," and they will respect you for it but will still be a little dubious.

Pour the eggs from the blender into a nonstick pan that is still very nonstick. Don't use the old hand-me-down nonstick that your mom gave you from her kitchen when you moved into your first apartment and she wanted a new one. Use a nice nonstick pan that you take good care of that doesn't actually let anything stick to it. Add the butter and salt and put it on the stove over medium-low heat.

Stir your eggs thoroughly with a heatproof rubber spatula until the eggs just start to set. Now stir much slower so that you allow curds to develop. Scrambled eggs should have curds about the size of a quarter. We are not making those goofy French ones that look like cottage cheese; we are making something that looks like what your mom made for you when you were a kid. But the perfect version of that. If your eggs are setting so quickly that you think they will be finished before you read another sentence, then take them off of the stove now. You can cook these eggs as slowly as you want, but if you go too fast they will overcook. What you are looking for is quarter-size curds that are just coated in a glossy sheen. When you have reached that stage, put your eggs in a bowl and eat them with toast and write me a thank-you letter.

If they are for a sandwich, you can cook them just a tiny bit longer without stirring so that they set into what looks a little bit more like an omelet. In either case, I want to stress that the secret is not to add liquid, and it's not to undercook the eggs so that they are super wet; you just have to cook them gently, stir just the right amount, and take them off at the right time. Does that sound daunting? I wish I could show you how to do it but I am counting my stacks of royalty money in Barbados right now with my friend Dahren, and you are at home trying to scramble eggs for a woman who will leave you someday. I'm just kidding! I'm sure she will stay with you forever. Scrambled eggs over rice are particularly amazing.

Fried Broccoli

Makes enough for 4 to 6 sandwiches

There are a lot of fried things in this book! My apologies, but this is a book about sandwiches, and it is hard to ignore the fact that fried things are awesome on sandwiches. For me, having one fried component in an otherwise healthy sandwich is what sandwich dreams are made of. And there is a special place in my heart for fried broccoli, because it really is what started my career as a chef. I've always loved broccoli tempura. I would order the vegetable tempura at sushi restaurants but I would ask for just the broccoli because I love broccoli, and it turns out that broccoli tempura might actually be the best broccoli ever! So when I was working on the menu for No. 7, I knew that I wanted to do something with fried broccoli. I thought about the sesame oil that made the batter so special, and that took me to hummus, which made me think of dill, which somehow led me to grapefruit. Anyway, that's how we ended up with Fried Broccoli with Black Bean Hummus, Grapefruit, and Arugula and Dill Salad with Shallot Vinaigrette at No. 7, and it's the only dish that's been on the menu ever since we opened. And while a lot of what I was doing at the beginning was very derivative of the food I was cooking for Jean-Georges, that dish was of a style that I would develop over the years into what I like to think is now my own distinct style. Here's how you make the fried broccoli part of it.

Vegetable oil, for frying

½ cup all-purpose flour

¼ cup cornstarch

1 tablespoon kosher salt

1 teaspoon baking powder

1 teaspoon sesame oil

1½ teaspoons balsamic vinegar

1 large head of broccoli, bottom half of stem removed, cut into long florets

---

Put 3 inches of oil in a large saucepan, making sure there are a couple inches of clearance, and heat it over medium heat to 375°F on a candy/frying thermometer. (If you don't have one of those, just give up and go home. Or look and see if the oil looks really weirdly wavy inside and a bread crumb sizzles instantly when you drop it in.)

In a medium mixing bowl, whisk together the flour, cornstarch, salt, and baking powder, then whisk in the sesame oil, balsamic vinegar, and ¾ cup of water until smooth to make the batter.

Line a plate with paper towels. Put all of the broccoli into the tempura batter and mix it around so that it is totally coated.

When the oil is ready, raise the heat to medium high. With a pair of tongs, pick up a piece of broccoli and let a little of the excess batter drain off. Put it three-fourths of the way into the oil and hold it there for 10 seconds. If you just drop it in, it will stick to the bottom and people will make fun of you. We've been made fun of enough, don't you think?

Repeat that process with a couple more pieces of broccoli and then let them fry for 1 to 2 minutes, flip them all, and then let them fry for another minute. When they are golden and gorgeous, remove them from the oil and let them drain on the paper towel–lined plate.

Working in batches, repeat this process with the rest of the broccoli. Francis, what should I do here? This is basically the same recipe as the eggplant. Maybe I'll fry the eggplant differently? `[We'll just make sure this recipe is far enough away from the eggplant so that no one will realize you're basically plagiarizing yourself. —Ed.]`

Broccoli Falafel

Makes enough for 6 to 8 falafel sandwiches

I really love falafel. It is one of the few vegetarian sandwiches that people around the world have truly embraced, and it is obvious why. It turns out that having something fried in a sandwich, even if it's a yucky vegetable, is just as awesome as having a chunk of meat in a sandwich. Unfortunately it's probably not that much healthier than any meat that's not, say, pork belly, but really, what is so exciting about healthy anyway? And I mean that in all seriousness. What is so incredibly important about being healthy? I see the point in not being super unhealthy or sick, but what's wrong with just being a regular, slightly overweight, moderate drinking, no exercise, eats-something-deep-fried-every-day person? You don't go to the gym, but you also don't go to the doctor. That's life. I think that you should eat more falafel. It's got fiber, I guess.

4 cups chopped broccoli (1 large or 2 small heads, stems and all)

½ cup all-purpose flour

2 garlic cloves

½ onion, roughly chopped

Pinch of red chile flakes

½ teaspoon ground coriander

1 teaspoon ground cumin

½ cup chopped fresh cilantro

2 teaspoons kosher salt, plus more to taste

Vegetable oil, for frying

In a food processor, combine the broccoli, flour, garlic, onion, chile flakes, coriander, cumin, cilantro, and 2 teaspoons of salt. Process until smooth and then refrigerate for an hour. This will allow the flour to fully hydrate and become a binding agent, which will keep the falafel from being too crumbly.

Form the broccoli mixture into balls, using 2 tablespoons of the stuff per ball.

Heat 3 inches of oil in a large Dutch oven over medium-high heat to 350°F on a candy/frying thermometer. (If you don't have one of those, get several and give them out as gifts. Or look and see if the oil looks kinda wavy inside and a bit of broccoli mixture sizzles instantly when you drop it in.)

Working in batches so there's some room between the balls, fry the falafel, turning occasionally, for 3 to 4 minutes or until quite dark on the outside. Remove them with a slotted spoon and drain well on paper towels.

Fried Squid

Makes enough fried squid for 4 to 6 sandwiches, or 1 order of calamari to be doused with lemon and salt and consumed, possibly with Marinara Sauce (page 166)

I am just ████████ ████████ ████████ ████████ ████████ I haven't done that ████████ ████████ ████████ ████████ at 9 pm and I slept ████████ ████████ which should be really ████████ am worried that I won't enjoy it a ton.

Vegetable oil, for frying

½ pound squid, cleaned, eyes and beak removed, heads cut in half lengthwise and tubes cut into ½-inch rings

1 tablespoon kosher salt

1 cup all-purpose flour

████████ Heat 3 inches of oil in a large saucepan over medium-high heat to 350°F.

Toss the squid with the salt and then the flour.

Fry the squid. I don't even know what it means to be a chef anymore.

[Sorry, Tyler's not feeling well. Maybe you should just follow the frying step for the fried clams on page 146, or really any one of the other fried recipes in this book. It's basically the same thing. The squid are done when they're light golden and just firm, so drain them on paper towels then and finish them with a little salt. —Ed.]

SAUCES

Mayo

Grape Jelly Mayo, a.k.a. Genius Russian Dressing

Michelada Mayo

Jalapeño Mayo

Actual Russian Dressing

Smoked French Dressing

Black Bean Hummus

Special Sauce

Fort Greene Goddess Dressing

Old Bay Curry Sauce

Shallot-Ginger Vinaigrette

Marinara Sauce

Bacon Mayo (for Vegetarians and Meat Eaters)

No.7 Steak Sauce

Leche de Tigre Mayo

Pho Mayo

Tartar Sauce

Dirty Tartar Sauce

Roasted Tomato Mayo

Mayo

Makes 1 pint of mayo!

You can make mayo! That said, you definitely do not *need* to make mayo. You can buy a bunch of different kinds, and they are all awesome. Hellmann's is the standard, and I love it; Kewpie is a Japanese brand that has sugar and MSG, and it is incredible; and there will always be room in my fridge for Miracle Whip, because there is honestly nothing quite like Miracle Whip. What I'm trying to say is that if you think that you are making your own mayo because it will make you better than people who love these time-tested, world-beloved sauces, then you are a jerk and you should know that people find you annoying. If you're making your own mayo because you want to know every ingredient that goes into your body, then I want to know who you are and why you are so important to the Earth, because unless your name is John Connor, Sarah Connor, or Kyle Reese, and you have to stay strong for a rebellion against Skynet, I don't see why you can't just eat food like a person and stop worrying so much about every little detail. I mean, does anybody really feel good ever? Is there such a thing as not being tired and achy, or not having an upset stomach all of the time? If you answered yes to those questions, then I don't think you're drinking enough or your life is too easy and you should try drinking more. But I know that you're making your own mayo because you already have the ingredients in your fridge, you own one of those little immersion blenders, and you want to make every ingredient in your sandwich from scratch. And I think that's great. I'm sorry that I got mad before.

1 egg yolk

1½ tablespoons white vinegar

1 tablespoon Dijon mustard

1 teaspoon kosher salt

1 teaspoon sugar

1½ cups vegetable oil

In a medium mixing bowl, whisk together the egg yolk, vinegar, mustard, salt, sugar, and 1 tablespoon water until fully dissolved and combined.

Place a damp towel under the bowl so that when you whisk, the bowl stays still without you having to hold it. Now whisk like a wild animal.

With your free hand, very slowly drizzle the vegetable oil into the bowl, continuing to whisk until all of the oil is incorporated. If you poured your oil in too fast, you will know it and you will want to cry into your broken mayo a little. Do it. The extra water will help you save it. Or if you don't have tears to cry anymore, add a teaspoon of water to it, grab another bowl, and very slowly drizzle your broken mess into it while whisking like you've lost control of your arm. It should come together. Then slowly add the rest of the oil while whisking.

Alternatively, you can just dump all of the ingredients in a pint glass, insert an immersion blender, turn it on, and slowly pull it out of the glass, making mayo as you go. That is what we do at No. 7 Sub, but we use a really big pint glass and a really big immersion blender. This will keep in the refrigerator for three or four days.

You can add awesome things to this basic mayo recipe to make some super-fun flavored mayos.

Grape Jelly Mayo, a.k.a. Genius Russian Dressing

Makes 1 cup

You just read the name of this recipe and I know that you're afraid of it, but you need to embrace your fear and make this and eat it. This is like a super-quick Russian dressing. Really. Did you ever see *Defending Your Life*? It's about overcoming fear and meeting Glenn Close and Rip Torn and going to heaven. You have to use at least 20 percent of your brain to fully understand this sauce, but even with less, it's still awesome.

¾ cup Mayo (PAGE 160)

¼ cup grape jelly

Kosher salt to taste

Mix the mayo and jelly together thoroughly. It will be speckled like a beautiful Easter egg. Taste and add enough salt to make it savory if necessary. I often find that the salt isn't really necessary, but it's helpful if the idea of mixing mayo and jelly freaks you out and you want to feel like you have some control over the situation. Stored in a container with a tight-fitting lid, this will keep forever if you used store-bought mayo, or a week or so if you made the mayo.

Michelada Mayo

Makes 1¼ cups

This is a loose sauce. You could cook down the beer to concentrate it and chill it before adding to the mayo to keep the mayo more mayo-like in texture, but it will lose some of its beer appeal. Messy sandwiches are a part of life, and it is better to embrace them than to get all Felix Unger about it.

1 cup Mayo (PAGE 160)

1 tablespoon Tabasco sauce

1 teaspoon lime juice

¼ cup beer (something with a lot of color and flavor, but not a lot of hops; Negra Modelo would work well here), reduced to 1 tablespoon if you must

Mix thoroughly. Refrigerate in a small container with a tight-fitting lid and this will last three or four days and make you feel so proud every time you eat a sandwich.

Jalapeño Mayo

Makes a little less than 2 cups

This is so easy, and everybody gets so excited about it. You could just put mayo and jalapeños on a sandwich, and if you're by yourself, maybe just do that. But when I put jalapeño mayo on a sandwich at the sub shop, I win awards. Not James Beard awards, because I am not that kind of winner. I hope that didn't sound bitter, because I am many things but bitter is not one of them. I think "stupid" sums up all of those things pretty nicely, just like putting jalapeños into the mayo is simpler to explain to people and makes them more comfortable.

2 jalapeños, stems discarded*

1½ cups Mayo (PAGE 160)

* If you want it to be less spicy you can remove the seeds too, but if you don't like spicy food, then why are you making jalapeño mayo? I'm not trying to be rude, I just don't think you're really thinking this through.

Turn on a gas burner to high. If you have an electric stove, then you are ridiculous. Put this book down and decide if you're really serious about this whole "cooking" thing. Nobody will be surprised if you just quit now. I have always known that you get really excited about things and then drop them as soon as they get hard. Put the jalapeños on the burner and burn them until they are evenly black on all sides, about 1 minute per side, turning them with tongs.

Or, if you didn't quit when I was giving you a hard time before (I knew you would pull through!), you could put your jalapeños in a roasting pan under a broiler so hot it could melt the evil T-1000 and burn your jalapeños that way.

Put your burnt jalapeños (don't scrape off the burnt stuff) in a food processor with the mayo and process until smooth. Store in a small container with a tight-fitting lid in the refrigerator until you've eaten all of it, three or four days have passed, or you are told otherwise by somebody who knows more about food safety than me.

Actual Russian Dressing

Makes about 1½ cups

To me, Russian dressing should taste like everything you want to put on a hamburger already mixed together. It is one of the greatest sandwich condiments of all time, but I've never actually dressed a salad with it. But I'm sure it makes an incredible salad. Something bitter like chopped chicory or red endive leaves tossed with Russian dressing, some breaded and fried chunks of herring, lemon zest, a ton of black pepper, and a tiny bit of Parmesan cheese. That would be great. But for now, let's just make the dressing.

½ cup Mayo (PAGE 160)

½ cup ketchup

1 tablespoon Tabasco sauce

½ cup chopped pickles, like Cucumber Muchim (see PAGE 69)

Mix thoroughly. Store in a small container with a tight-fitting lid. It keeps in the refrigerator for three or four days.

Smoked French Dressing

Makes 2 cups

People use the term *crack* a lot when talking about food. Chefs name dishes after it to imply that their bananas Foster is so good that you will steal from your family to be able to eat it. And customers say things like "You must put crack in this food" to imply that they may call the police because they think I am ruining whole communities' lives. How disturbing is that? I wish nobody would ever say that to me again. ~~But if they do I'm going to tell them that I put the flu virus in their food. Readers of the Post-Apocalyptic Future: I am so sorry. This book was supposed to be published in 2015, but due to arguments about photography (I wanted pictures of people dressed up like broccoli punching cows in the face and Clarkson Potter thought that was too "random") this book didn't appear on shelves until 2016, too late to stop the "LeBron Flu" that decimated humanity and left you with this terrible book as your only way of remembering life in the pre-flu world.~~ `[This is too random. —Ed.]`

½ cup ketchup

1 garlic clove, minced

½ tablespoon Dijon mustard

½ cup Mayo (PAGE 160)

½ cup white vinegar

1 tablespoon honey

1 teaspoon salt

½ cup canola oil

Equipment: Smoker (PAGE 163)

Handful of mesquite chips for smoking

So you're going to smoke some ketchup now. It will not get you high, but it will make everything you put it on taste like a really awesome hot dog. A smoker is actually just an enclosed space where you can generate smoke from wood chips, letting that smoke pass over your food and then escape. There is "hot smoking," like with barbecue or kielbasa, where you are trying to maintain a specific temperature so that the food cooks slowly while you smoke it, and there is "cold smoking," like for smoked salmon, where the food should stay cold so that it doesn't cook while smoking. But we are smoking ketchup like crazy people, and we don't really need to worry about the temperature of our smoker. So, to that end, you could put a lit charcoal briquette on a baking sheet, put a small pile of wood chips on top of it, put a dish of ketchup a few inches away from it, and cover the whole thing with a box, using a stick that's taller than the box to hold it up at one end like you are trying to catch a cartoon rabbit. Do a Google Images search for "cartoon rabbit trap" and you will see a few examples. But if you have time to just google that anyway, maybe google "how to set up a smoker" and let the Internet explain it better than I can.

Put your ketchup in something made of nonreactive metal, place it in the smoker, smoke it until the smoke runs out, remove your dank-and-smoky ketchup, and cool it down.

Or you could buy liquid smoke. Nobody likes to talk about liquid smoke, but it's honestly not such a bad thing. It's made by quickly chilling smoke so that it condenses and mixing it with water. You then put that liquid in things. If you use too much, your food will taste like cheap ham because they use hickory smoke for liquid smoke, and hickory smoke alone makes everything taste like cheap ham. If you use liquid smoke, just pour a few drops into the cup of ketchup (be careful because that stuff is powerful!).

Or if you don't want to set up a smoker or use liquid smoke, you could add 2 teaspoons of Lapsang souchong tea leaves to the ketchup. It tastes like a campfire in the best way possible. It's probably your best bet if you don't want to use a smoker or liquid smoke.

Put the smoked ketchup along with the rest of the dressing ingredients in a blender and puree until smooth. This will keep in the refrigerator for a week or so.

Black Bean Hummus

Makes 2 cups

If you are looking for an authentic hummus recipe, then why are you holding this book and reading this recipe right now? Go get a real cookbook that will teach you real things. This hummus has many of the ingredients usually associated with hummus, but the amounts are all screwy and it's too sweet. All that said, this hummus makes one hell of a good sandwich condiment, as well as being pretty excellent in a double-decker broccoli taco! Don't get too hung up on authenticity, or you will end up being disappointed a lot. That last statement is about life, not just food.

¼ cup black sesame seeds

1¼ cups drained cooked black beans, cooking liquid reserved*

Juice of 1 lemon (about 3 tablespoons)

2 tablespoons tahini

2 teaspoons sugar

1 garlic clove, minced

1 teaspoon kosher salt

* Or you can use canned beans, but save the goo from the can (and you might have to add a little water).

In a small sauté pan, sauté the black sesame seeds over high heat for 2 minutes, or until hot to the touch and very fragrant.

Put the sesame seeds, beans, 1 cup of the bean cooking liquid, lemon juice, tahini, sugar, garlic, and salt in a food processor and process until smooth. If you have a fancy blender with a plunger, you could make the hummus in that and it will be much smoother, but who actually has one of those at home? This keeps, in an airtight container in the fridge, for four or five days.

Special Sauce

Makes about 2 cups

What's so special about this sauce? Absolutely nothing, I just couldn't come up with a better name. That said, it is delicious. And not just on sandwiches. Use it as a dip for potato chips or shrimp cocktail, or just eat it with a spoon, you weirdo. #food #foodsauce #chef #sauce #specialcheffoodsauce (I just wanted to have some hashtags in my print book so that this book will always be relevant.)

1 cup Mayo (PAGE 160)

½ cup whole-grain mustard

½ cup sweet chili sauce

1 cup dill sprigs, chopped

Mix thoroughly. Keep refrigerated in a plastic container with a tight-fitting lid and use this sauce for everything. At the original No. 7 in Fort Greene we currently serve this sauce as a dip for fried baby artichokes and it is totally excellent. It will keep three or four days, longer if your mayo is store-bought.

Fort Greene Goddess Dressing

Makes 1½ cups

I always thought that green goddess dressing was something that hippies ate while sitting in a circle, banging on djembe drums, and reading *The Mists of Avalon*. It turns out that it's super old, older than hippies, and has anchovies in it. Hippies almost never eat anchovies!

My restaurant is in a neighborhood called Fort Greene. (How come nobody but me thinks it's funny that the park across the street is actually called Cuyler Gore Park?)

½ garlic clove

2 sprigs mint, stems removed

4 sprigs dill

4 sprigs parsley

2 sprigs basil, stems removed

½ cup buttermilk

¼ cup Mayo (PAGE 160)

1 tablespoon lemon juice

½ teaspoon kosher salt

1 anchovy fillet

½ cup canola oil

Combine the garlic, mint, dill, parsley, basil, buttermilk, mayo, lemon juice, salt, anchovy, and oil in a blender and puree until smooth. I would have just written, "Put everything in a blender and puree," but Clarkson Potter wanted me to write everything out. [I let "mix everything thoroughly" slide for all the other recipes. Just give me this once, to show you gave at least a quarter of a damn about our house style. —Ed. Also, now it looks like the copyeditor went through and added all the ingredients to all the times you said "mix everything thoroughly" anyway, so I'm sorry I was huffy before. —Ed.] Francis, do you ever feel like no matter how hard you work on a project, you're going to feel equally sad when it's over? I mean, right when you finish, if you've really done your best, that's a super feeling, but then a week later, it's the same. No? Like, the other day I decided that I should move to Coney Island, because if I'm going to be stuck in New York City, I might as well live by the beach. And I can open a tofu-dog stand on the beach and not work super hard and swim a lot so that I sleep well. But will that be any better? The hardest thing about owning a restaurant is owing people money. Nobody really talks about that, but you are constantly in debt to people, be it vendors, investors, the IRS, you name it. If I ever manage to not owe anyone anything, or at least to owe less to people, I am going to fake my own death, change my name to Felix, and move to Venezuela and open a beachside stand selling *perros de tofu* and hand-bottled water. So if I owe you money and I die, don't go looking for me in Venezuela. I'm too clever to do that after writing it in this book. Right? ;) [I don't want this book to end either, Tyler. —Ed.]

The dressing keeps for about a week in the fridge.

Old Bay Curry Sauce

*Makes about 4 cups, which is kind of a lot for home, to be honest**

Old Bay Seasoning and Tony Chachere's Original Creole Seasoning are basically American curry powders. They're both completely awesome and delicious, and you should own a jar of both. Coconut milk curries made with alternative spice blends are a thing that should probably be more popular.

* You could cut this in half, but every time I have ever used half a can of coconut milk, I always forget to use the rest and end up having to throw it away. So think about your week and plan accordingly. You can use this like a curry sauce and cook some chickpeas and cauliflower in it and serve it over rice!

3 tablespoons olive oil

5 garlic cloves, roughly chopped

1½ tablespoons Old Bay Seasoning

4 lime leaves, bruised (optional)

1 28-ounce can whole peeled tomatoes (get the good San Marzano ones)

1 13.5-ounce can coconut milk

Kosher salt to taste

Heat the olive oil in a medium saucepan over medium heat. Add the garlic, Old Bay, and lime leaves and cook, stirring until everything is nicely toasted, about 2 minutes. Add the canned tomatoes, bring up to a boil, reduce the heat, and simmer until really thick, about 30 to 40 minutes.

Puree the sauce in a blender, being careful to leave a gap in the lid so that steam can escape. Start slow and gradually increase the speed so that the sauce doesn't jump out and burn your face. This sauce is incredible, but not worth destroying your face for. Puree for a couple of minutes to get the sauce as smooth as possible.

Strain the sauce through a fine-mesh strainer to get rid of any tiny bits of lime leaf.

Add the coconut milk, add salt to taste, and chill the sauce. This should keep for about a week, covered in the refrigerator.

Shallot-Ginger Vinaigrette

Makes ¾ cup

I wanted to make carrot-ginger dressing for sandwiches but people associate carrot-ginger dressing with sushi restaurants so they acted like that was weird. But there really aren't any rules in cooking, I think that people just pretend there are to scare you out of trying amazing things so that they can always get all of the compliments at dinner parties. It's like when people tell you that baking is a science. Does anybody really believe that? I mean, there is science involved, but there is also science involved in savory cooking, driving a car, and watching TV. Weighing sugar on a scale does not make baking cookies anything like working to cure a disease or trying to figure out climate change. This shallot-ginger vinaigrette however, especially when applied to a veggie burger with crispy pepperoni and avocado, may in fact be the cure for some kind of disease.

1 shallot, roughly chopped

1 1-inch piece ginger, sliced into ¼-inch coins

½ garlic clove

½ cup apple cider vinegar

1 tablespoon canola oil

½ tablespoon honey

½ teaspoon kosher salt

In a blender, combine the shallot, ginger, garlic, vinegar, canola oil, honey, and salt and blend on high until smooth. This will keep for a month in the refrigerator, but try to eat it faster than that.

Marinara Sauce

Makes a little less than 4 cups

I call this marinara sauce because I love the word *marinara*, but it's just a super-simple tomato sauce. My recipe has no onions because, as much as I love onions all of the time, I don't love them in my tomato sauce. And it's barely cooked, because that's also how I like it. But if you prefer onions and long cooking times, then you are like most people in the world, so go ahead and express yourself. When I first started cooking professionally, people always wanted to tell me about their recipe for tomato sauce upon hearing that I was a cook. Those recipes always involved red wine, onions, and sugar, and I'm certain they were all delicious. I think that now, thanks to the Internet, everybody who is interested in cooking knows a lot about making tomato sauce and there are message boards to discuss it, and nobody needs to tell me about it. I kind of miss those days.

2 teaspoons kosher salt, plus more to taste

1 28-ounce can whole peeled tomatoes in tomato puree

2 tablespoons olive oil

3 garlic cloves, sliced thin

Add 2 teaspoons salt to the canned tomatoes and puree them with one of those little immersion blenders. Or, if you don't have one of those, put the salt and tomatoes in a blender and puree on low speed until smooth but not aerated. Or you can put the salt and tomatoes in a bowl and crush them by hand.

In a medium saucepan, heat the olive oil over medium heat. Once the oil is shimmering hot but not quite smoking, add the garlic and cook, stirring constantly, until the garlic is lightly browned. It may help to tilt the pan so that the olive oil remains deep enough to fry the garlic. `[I love doing this! No one ever writes it into their recipes! —Ed.]` This will take about 2 minutes.

Add the tomatoes, turn up the heat to high and, stirring occasionally, bring the sauce to a full boil. Once the sauce boils, it's ready. Taste it and add more salt to if you want it, then cool it down or put it on a sandwich. This will keep for a week in the refrigerator.

Bacon Mayo (for Vegetarians and Meat Eaters)

Makes 1½ cups

Sometimes you want to put bacon on a sandwich, but then you realize that you are vegetarian. This is not quite like putting bacon on a sandwich, because it won't have the texture of bacon. But it will taste like bacon. And if you make it with Vegenaise, then you have vegan Bacon Mayo!

2 teaspoons Lapsang souchong tea leaves

1½ cups Mayo (PAGE 160)

½ teaspoon ground allspice

½ teaspoon ground black pepper

1 garlic clove, finely minced

1 teaspoon grape jelly

2 tablespoons low-sodium soy sauce

Preheat an oven to 250°F and toast the tea leaves for 10 minutes or until completely dry and crumbly. Crush into a powder.

In a medium mixing bowl, combine the mayo, tea powder, allspice, black pepper, garlic, grape jelly, and soy sauce. Whisk until thoroughly combined. Taste the mayo. It totally does not taste like bacon.

Put the mayo in the fridge and let it sit there for at least an hour and up to three or four days. Now taste the mayo. Bacon! Kind of! But definitely delicious.

No. 7 Steak Sauce

Makes 1¼ cups

One night at No. 7 somebody asked for steak sauce. I thought that was really weird because everything we serve already has a sauce because we are French like that. I'm not the kind of chef who is insulted by people wanting to put ketchup on everything (I *do* think it's weird that some people want everything they eat to taste exactly the same, but it works for dogs and cats, so who am I to judge?), but it just seemed like such a strange request that I didn't know what to do. Luckily Katherine told me to mix General Tso's Sauce with ketchup, and not only was the customer very happy but also No. 7 Steak Sauce was born!

½ cup General Tso's Sauce (PAGE 82)

½ cup ketchup

¼ cup Mayo (PAGE 160) (optional)

Mix together the General Tso's sauce, ketchup, and mayo and serve. You can omit the mayo if you want this sauce to be super intense, but I prefer ketchup that has mayo mixed into it. In fact, I think it's a little strange that people eat straight ketchup because it is so intense. But people seem to find it strange that I don't drink water, and I think that those things may be related. This keeps for about a week in the refrigerator.

Leche de Tigre Mayo

Makes enough mayo to party all night long (about 1½ cups)

Leche de tigre is the marinating liquid from your ceviche. It literally means "tiger's milk," and it supposedly makes your dick (or lady-dick—this book is for everyone) hard. I'm not sure that leche de tigre is going to enhance your sexuality in any way, but I do know that it's crazy delicious. That said, it's straight liquid, so be advised: When you mix it with your mayonnaise, it will make it loose, and loose mayo makes for a messy sandwich. But your dick (or lady-dick) is hard, so why do you care if your sandwich is messy?

½ cup leche de tigre from Ceviche (PAGE 97)

1 cup Mayo (PAGE 160)

Combine ingredients and try to control the beast that you've just awoken inside of you. This will maintain function for two to three days in the fridge.

Pho Mayo

Makes 1¼ cups

This is basically a recipe for pho, everyone's favorite Vietnamese noodle soup, but instead of adding beef bones and spices and water and then boiling it for hours, we are just going to mix all the seasonings for pho together and then eat it on a sandwich. I just googled "pho mayo" to make sure that it doesn't already exist, and it turns out there is a town called Mayo in Maryland and they have some Vietnamese restaurants. Actually, Mayo Beach Park looks really beautiful. See, we are learning together!! Also, please don't be disappointed when you realize that there is no raw beef in this recipe. [OMFG TYLER WHY DOES THIS REALLY TASTE LIKE PHO ARE YOU A GOD —Ed.] I'm really more like Achilles in that my mother is a goddess, I have one secret weakness but am otherwise indestructible, and I can make mayonnaise bend to my will using only my mind because Achilles could do that. Homer doesn't really get into it though.

¼ yellow onion

1½-inch piece of ginger, cut in half lengthwise

½ cinnamon stick

1 piece star anise

½ teaspoon fennel seeds

4 whole cloves

1 tablespoon maple syrup

1 teaspoon fish sauce or salt, to taste

1 cup Mayo (PAGE 160)

Hold the onion with a pair of tongs and burn for 3 to 4 minutes directly over the flame of a burner, until blackened all over. Do the same with the ginger. You may also do this under the broiler, but it will take longer. Let them cool and then put them in a blender with the cinnamon, star anise, fennel seed, cloves, maple syrup, and fish sauce, and puree until smooth. Add the mayo. If you're worried about eating small chunks of cinnamon, pass this through a fine-mesh sieve. Store in a plastic container with a tight-fitting lid for three or four days in the refrigerator.

Tartar Sauce

Makes about 2½ cups

Tartar sauce blah blah blah.

1 egg yolk

1 ripe avocado

1 tablespoon kosher salt

1 tablespoon sugar

2 tablespoons malt vinegar

½ jalapeño, seeds optional depending on how spicy you want this to be

1 cup sliced pickles, preferably Cucumber Muchim (see PAGE 69), squeezed to get rid of excess juice

½ cup fresh tarragon leaves

A few drops of liquid smoke or 1 teaspoon loose Lapsang souchong tea leaves

1 cup vegetable oil

In a food processor, combine the egg yolk, avocado, salt, sugar, vinegar, jalapeño, pickles, tarragon, and the liquid smoke. Process until everything is evenly chopped and then drizzle the oil in very slowly to emulsify. This will keep for a few days in the refrigerator, but because of the avocado, it will turn brown pretty quickly, so try to make this the day you plan on eating it.

Dirty Tartar Sauce

Makes about 1½ cups

Dirty tartar sauce is stupid.

½ cup chicken livers

½ teaspoon salt

1 tablespoon vegetable oil

½ recipe Tartar Sauce (PREVIOUS RECIPE)

Pat the chicken livers very dry with paper towels and season them on both sides with the salt.

Heat the oil in a large sauté pan over high heat. When the oil in the pan begins to smoke, carefully place the livers in the pan, making sure there is an inch or so around each one so that they don't steam. Sauté hard on the one side until the livers are cooked most of the way through and really browned, about 5 minutes, then flip them, finish cooking them on the other side for about a minute, and then transfer them to a plate to cool. Once they are cool, roughly chop them and add them to the tartar sauce. Like the regular tartar sauce, this will change color after a day, so try to eat this all the day you make it.

Roasted Tomato Mayo

Makes about 1½ cups of setting off your smoke alarm for the greater good of sandwiches

This is essentially a recipe for a cooked tomato salsa, but instead of adding a tiny bit of sour cream to mellow it out, we are going to add a whole bunch of mayonnaise because we want to make people happy and sometimes a little extra mayo is all it takes.

1 medium tomato, quartered

½ small yellow onion, quartered

¼ jalapeño, cut in half, seeds unmolested

1 garlic clove, cut in half lengthwise

1 teaspoon olive oil

2 teaspoons kosher salt

½ cup Mayo (PAGE 160)

1 teaspoon white vinegar

Heat the oven as hot as it will go. While it is heating, put a large, rimmed roasting pan into the oven to get as hot as it can possibly get.

Toss the tomato, onion, jalapeño, and garlic in a small mixing bowl with the olive oil and salt.

When the oven is super hot, open the door, pull out your roasting pan, and unceremoniously dump your tomato salad into the pan. The pan will protest, but what can it do? Give the pan a shake so that your fruits and veggies spread out into a single layer, but don't stir things around too much. We want to achieve color without actually cooking this food too much and if you stir a lot then the tomatoes will start releasing water and it will take a lot more cooking to achieve browning. Also know that it is completely okay if some of the food burns a little. No, I won't even be upset if the garlic burns because I am open-minded and I love food.

Put the roasting pan back in the oven and cook for 6 to 8 minutes, undisturbed. When you pull the pan out it should look a little brown and black on the edges and awesome throughout. If you didn't get any color, feel free to throw the whole thing under the broiler for a couple of minutes. Let the pan rest and what is left of the juice in the tomatoes and onions should come out and help you deglaze the pan a little. Transfer the roasted tomato mix to a smaller container and chill the fuck out while this chills completely in the refrigerator.

When the tomatoes are cool, add the mayo and vinegar and puree until smooth. This is supposed to be loose, so don't get freaked out if it doesn't look thick enough to you. This makes one of the best things you could ever dip a french fry into.

MISCELLANEOUS

Grape & Celery Salad

Roasted Onions

Pickled Red Onions

Roasted Sweet Potatoes

Pickled Blueberries

Pickled Mushrooms

Fried Shallots

Pico de Lettuce

Pickled Jalapeños

Raisin & Scallion Relish

Spaghetti Squash Salad

Haricots Verts Salad

Fried Garlic

Shredded Cabbage Salad

Avocado Blue Cheese

Jicama Salad

Pickled Bean Sprouts

Coleslaw

Basic Potato Chips

BBQ Potato Chip Spice Mix

Grape & Celery Salad

Makes enough for 8 to 10 sandwiches or 2 awesome salads

This recipe is meant to add a little taste of Oscar Tschirky's Waldorf salad to any sandwich when it wants to feel more like old New York. I wasn't born in New York, but I'm officially trapped here—for better or for worse. I came here for a girl, and I got stuck, opening businesses, convincing my family to move here, and now I can't leave. It took a few years for me to really embrace this city, but now I can't imagine living anywhere else. Except for when my friends who live in other places call and talk about how comfortable their lives are. If I were to live anywhere else, it would probably be Tulum, Mexico. Or maybe Salt Lake City. But I've grown to love living on Flatbush Avenue and falling asleep to the sound of cars honking their horns and people shouting. It's super relaxing to hear chaos outside but to know that my door is locked and I am comfortably in bed. And I've never actually been to the Waldorf Astoria.

2 cups grapes, halved and seeded (I vote green)

2 stalks celery, sliced thin against the fibers

½ small red onion, sliced thin

2 tablespoons white vinegar

1 tablespoon olive oil

1 teaspoon kosher salt, plus more if needed

Combine the grapes, celery, onion, vinegar, olive oil, and salt in a mixing bowl.Taste to check the seasoning and add more salt if necessary.

This will last for at least a week in the fridge, though it will get progressively uglier as the days go by. But it's going on a sandwich, hiding its flaws between bread, so who cares?

Roasted Onions

Makes 3 cups

Roasted onions are great because they're sweet and they refuse to sit down and be quiet. Be careful how you use roasted onions because they can completely take over, but used in the right places, caramelized onions can turn a regular sandwich into fireworks. But seriously, no more caramelized onions on burgers. It's like putting cheese and bacon on them burgers, and you know how I feel about that.

2 large onions, yellow or red, peeled and sliced into ½-inch rings

1 tablespoon olive or vegetable oil

2 teaspoons kosher salt

Preheat the oven to 450°F.

In a medium mixing bowl, toss the onions, oil, and salt together until thoroughly mixed. Don't worry about trying to separate all of the rings. Some will separate and some won't when you mix them, and I like the variety of having some cook more than others.

Place the onions on a baking sheet or a roasting pan and cook until somewhat tender and a little burnt, about 20 minutes. We're not really going for that melty oniony goo, which I definitely love, but we want the onions to still have a little bite so that they are a component of a sandwich, not a condiment. Picture the onions on a shish kebab, charred on the outside and still a little raw in the center. At some point somebody decided that we could only have onions that are raw or cooked to mush. But I like the in-between onions the best! This should not look super beautiful; some will be super dark, and the rings that stayed together will be less cooked. Variety is the spice in this dish. Transfer to a container and let cool before serving.

Will keep for five days in the refrigerator.

Pickled Red Onions

Makes 3 to 4 cups

After cucumbers, a red onion is probably the best thing you can pickle. It says so in the ~~Bible~~ Constitution! This is a quick and simple pickle that's perfect for sandwiches because it will punch through any ingredient and shout, "Vinegar! And fucking onions!!!"

2 red onions, halved and sliced thin

1 cup white vinegar

1 teaspoon kosher salt

Combine everything in a plastic container with a tight-fitting lid. Shake vigorously like you hate pickled red onions. Let sit for at least 30 minutes, but preferably for longer, shaking occasionally. These will last for a very long time in your fridge.

Roasted Sweet Potatoes

Makes 1 pound

I first had roasted sweet potatoes on a sandwich when I was in Lima, Peru. It was early in the morning, and I stumbled into a little place called Sandwich.com, which, by the way, is an incredible name for a sandwich shop. They had roast pork sandwiches with sweet potato, and they were radical. A few days later I was walking through a big stinky market in Huaraz, Peru, which is way up north, and I saw a bunch of sandwich shops. I went back in the afternoon to get a sandwich but couldn't find any of the sandwich shops. I asked several people (in Spanish mind you—my Spanish is pretty decent), and they all looked at me like I had asked where to buy black-market babies. Eventually I convinced somebody to explain to me what was going on, because everyone was acting like I was crazy for even asking about the sandwiches, and they said that, in Peru, sandwiches are only eaten for breakfast. Peru, my first question is, was that so fucking hard? You know what a sandwich is and you know what a sandwich shop is, but when somebody asks for the location of a sandwich shop that is closed for the day, you just clam up? If you come to New York and ask me where the Hustler Club is at 10 a.m., I'm going to tell you. And secondly, who arbitrarily decided that sandwiches are only for fucking breakfast? Do you turn into gremlins? Anyway, the following day I had another sandwich with sweet potatoes for breakfast, because I am not some kind of animal who eats a sandwich after the sun has fully risen in the sky, and it was awesome and I realized that it wasn't just a Sandwich.com thing, it's an awesome sandwich thing. It's like solid vegetable mayonnaise.

1 pound sweet potatoes, peeled and sliced into ½-inch disks

1 tablespoon olive or vegetable oil

1 teaspoon kosher salt

½ teaspoon smoked Spanish paprika

Preheat the oven to 375°F.

In a large mixing bowl, toss the sweet potatoes, oil, salt, and paprika together until thoroughly mixed.

Place the potatoes in one layer on a rimmed baking sheet and roast in the oven until tender and caramelized, about 30 minutes. Transfer to a container to cool. Will last for five days in the refrigerator.

Pickled Blueberries

Makes 1 quart, enough to share with all your friends who think it's weird to pickle blueberries

This is one of those things that makes everybody say, "Pickled blueberries? That's so crazy!" But, really, it's not very crazy. Lots of pickled things are secretly fruit: cucumbers, tomatoes, peppers. (What do they have to hide?) And more to the point, what is really so weird about pickling blueberries? This is a quick vinegar pickle, and the blueberries themselves never get super pickly on the inside, but the brine/blueberry/onion combo brings an excellent sweet-sourness to any sandwich. It's particularly good as a replacement for tomatoes. And they'll keep for a very long time in the fridge, so next time you see good, sweet blueberries at the farmers' market, buy a bunch of them and pickle away!

1 cup white vinegar, plus more if needed

¼ cup sugar

1¾ tablespoons kosher salt

1¼ pounds blueberries

1 small red onion, halved and thinly sliced

Combine everything in a plastic container with a tight-fitting lid. There should be enough vinegar to completely cover the berries and onions; if not, add a little more. Pretend that it is those pickled red onions that you hate so much and shake vigorously. You want to bruise the berries a little and also get out some of the aggression you feel toward your roommate. Why do you still have a roommate? Why do you hate pickled red onions so much? Let sit for at least 2 hours, but preferably longer, shaking occasionally. They will last in the refrigerator for a long time.

Pickled Mushrooms

Makes about 1 quart

This method of pickling mushrooms gives them the texture of those weird canned mushrooms they use at cheap pizza places. I love those canned mushrooms that they use at cheap pizza places. If you use a fancy mix of mushrooms, then this is like a really fancy version of those canned mushrooms that they use at cheap pizza places. I like all mushrooms, but for this I would be particularly inclined to use white buttons, criminis, or shiitakes, or if you have access to fancier

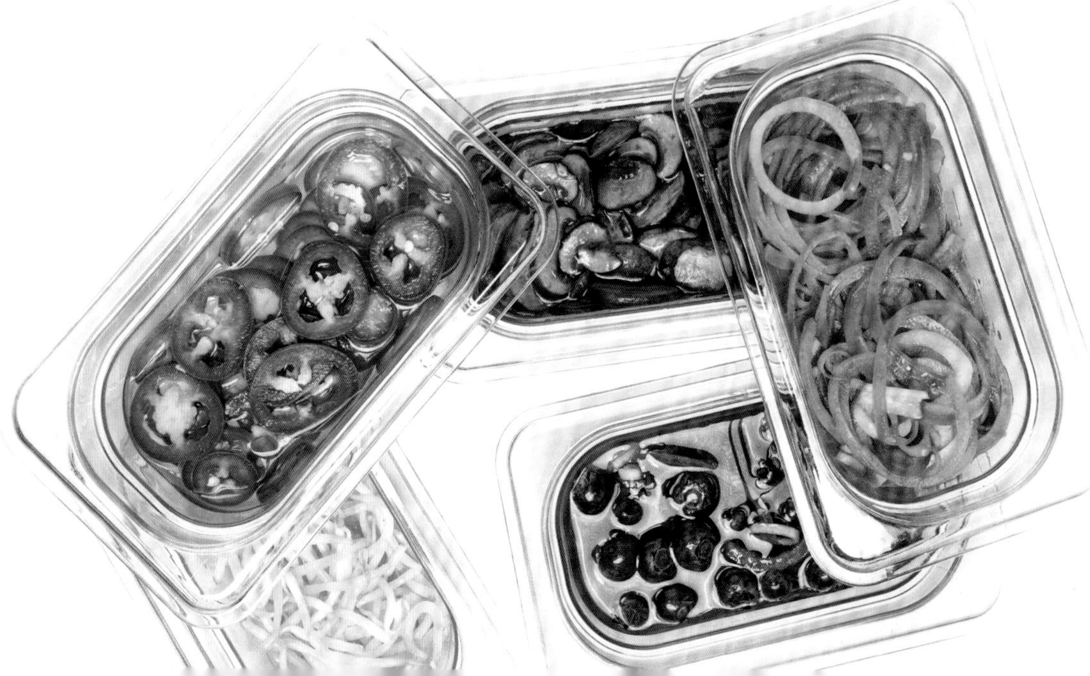

ones, maitakes or hon shimejis would be great too. Hon shimeji mushrooms, otherwise known as beech mushrooms, are one of the reasons that the Earth revolves around the sun. And just imagine if it didn't! You wouldn't be complaining about canned mushrooms at cheap pizza places then.

½ cup white or apple cider vinegar

½ teaspoon dried rosemary, crushed

½ teaspoon dried thyme

2 teaspoons kosher salt

1 pound mushrooms, any size, sliced thin

Combine the vinegar, rosemary, thyme, salt, and 1 cup of water in a small saucepan and bring to a boil over high heat.

Put the mushrooms in a mixing bowl big enough to hold the mushrooms and all of the liquid. Pour the liquid over the mushrooms. I know what you're thinking. This is not enough boiling liquid to actually cook 1 pound of mushrooms. You're right; it is not. We could have added more water to the pot, and then when we poured it over the mushrooms they would cook, but they would also give up their own water and we would end up with mushroom soup, and that's not what we're going for here. We just brought it to a boil to dissolve the salt and get the herbs super primed and ready. Now we're going to let the mixture sit in the bowl in the refrigerator, stirring very occasionally, for about 2 hours. At that point, all of the mushrooms should taste cooked and there should be enough liquid to more or less cover them. They will keep for a couple of weeks in the fridge, provided that you give the container a shake once in a while if the liquid doesn't fully cover the mushrooms.

Fried Shallots

Makes about a cup

Crispy, crunchy shallots are good for topping sandwiches, soups, scrambled eggs, ice cream, and just about anything else you can think of. I think fried shallots are in the bacon family in terms of their ability to add huge flavor to anything.

This recipe is for people who don't have a store where they can buy Southeast Asian fried shallots. If you do have such a store, then don't bother frying shallots at home, because they are way too delicious, and you will want to put them in and on everything. And then you'll be frying huge amounts of them and your apartment will smell like fried onions, and while you think that is awesome, your spouse or significant other might not be into that, and if you just had a huge jar of them from a store, then you could sneak them into all of your food, and nobody would say, "These onions are killing us!" and then move out. If you don't live in a place where you can buy them, then I suggest moving to a real city.

Backing up a minute, if your spouse or significant other moves out because you love frying shallots, then maybe there are bigger problems in your relationship and you should go to couples counseling. I tried that once and the counselor told my wife that I was a "waste of her ovaries," and then she threw a book at me and we got a divorce and I miss her. It was way bigger than fried shallots. Actually, she likes fried shallots. `[Tyler, you have an excellent new wife. I was at the wedding. It was literally five days ago. (Hi, Katherine!) —Ed.]`

Vegetable oil, for shallow frying

4 large shallots, sliced into ¼-inch rings (it is really helpful to have a Japanese mandoline for this)

1 teaspoon cornstarch

Kosher salt

Put an inch of oil in a medium saucepan and heat to around 225°F, or hot enough that a shallot ring sizzles gently a moment after you drop it in.

Set up a large plate lined with paper towels.

Toss the shallots with the cornstarch until the shallot rings are separated and everything feels dry. Put a quarter of the shallot slices in the oil and stir with a slotted spoon or wire spider. Cook until the shallot slices turn a blond color and immediately transfer the fried shallots to the paper towel–lined plate. Repeat the process until all of the shallots are fried.

Turn up the oil to 325°F, or hot enough to sizzle one of the already-fried shallot rings immediately when you drop it in.

Fry the shallots a second time, for about 10 to 20 seconds. You will see them puff up a little, and they will caramelize quickly, so don't let them go beyond light brown. Transfer the shallots back to the plate, but lined with new paper towels, and season with a little bit of salt.

The fried shallots will be awesome when cooled and can be stored in an airtight container for weeks. The fried shallot oil will also be awesome. Store that in the fridge.

Pico de Lettuce

Makes enough for 4 to 6 sandwiches

Most people are pretty sure that if you dress a salad too far in advance it will wilt and become disgusting and an embarrassment. But that is so arbitrary! We like wilted spinach. We like cucumber salad and coleslaw when they have been predressed and allowed to release a good bit of their water. It concentrates their flavors and gives them a very different, but no less awesome, texture. Well, I'm here to tell you that the same thing happens with lettuce, and we should embrace it, not throw it away and make a new salad! The thing is, a drained lettuce salad is one of the greatest sandwich condiments of all time. Instead of a big, unwieldy piece of lettuce, you can pack half a head of compressed lettuce on a sandwich, and think about what that means for the flavor of your sandwich! The only problem is marketing. Nobody wants to eat a sandwich with something called "old salad" on it, so in a fit of brilliance, I coined the term *Pico de Lettuce*. And I put it on the menu at the sub shops, and nobody seemed to notice. People talk about the sandwich

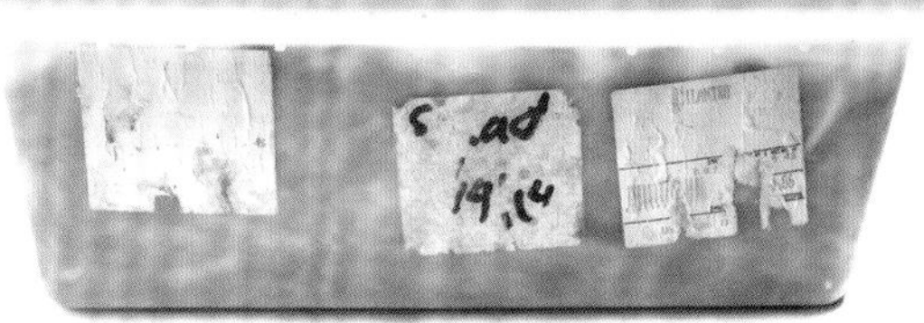

and act like they already know what Pico de Lettuce is. And they like it! But if they knew that it was just old salad they would probably be bummed. People can be so stupid. I am pretty stupid all of the time, so I'm not judging them. One time I drove to Boston by accident. I was crazy high on the weed. It was spring break, my freshman year of college—1997. Nobody makes mistakes like I do. I go big. Go big or go home. I went big, and then I went home, but it took a few extra hours because Boston is far from anything actually meaningful. Just kidding Boston, don't be so sensitive!!! (Francis, I am not kidding there, do you think that comes through?) [I do think it comes through, and I guess I shouldn't be psyched about the fact that we are going to sell zero copies of this book in the tenth-largest metropolitan area in the country, but maybe they will buy lots and lots of them to burn in the street. Keep it up. —Ed.]

1 head of romaine lettuce, cleaned, dried, and cut into ½-inch ribbons

1 garlic clove, minced

1 small red onion, sliced thin

Juice of ½ lemon

1 teaspoon white vinegar

1 teaspoon olive oil

½ teaspoon kosher salt

Combine the lettuce, garlic, onion, lemon juice, vinegar, olive oil, and salt in a medium mixing bowl. Let sit, stirring occasionally, for 30 minutes. Drain off most of the liquid and make the most interesting martini you've ever had. Store the Pico de Lettuce in the fridge, where it will keep for a week but, like many green things, will become less beautiful as the week progresses.

Pickled Jalapeños

Makes enough for 8 to 12 sandwiches

Pickled jalapeños are so stupid and delicious and easy that you should make them all of the time! And I'm not even talking about making a brine or anything; I'm talking about soaking jalapeños in vinegar and putting them on things. They'll add a pop to anything that needs a pop! I know a dude who needs a pop. He is a restaurant owner, and he is super nice to my face but apparently can't stop the flow of hate when my back is turned. I suspect it is because he has some issues, but I can't imagine that it's jealousy, as his restaurants are very successful and he's clearly very talented. Anyway, he said some horrible things about me to the ex-boyfriend of a girl that I was seriously in love with. We were dating until ex-boyfriend related the information to her. We got back together later, but that's another story entirely that we can talk about in some other cookbook, because this book is about sandwiches, so back to the topic at hand. See, restaurant-owner dude took everything out of context and made me look like a colossal jerk. I have been guilty of being a jerk, but really not this time. Anyway, sometimes I want to give him a pop of jalapeño juice in the eyes because he could at least have said what he had to say to my face. I even gave him a chance! I called him to say that I was super sorry if I had ever done anything to offend him, and he just acted like everything was cool! I don't understand people like that. (For the record, I wrote that intro in 2012 when I was pitching this book around. I'll leave it there for posterity's sake, but for the record, I am totally over that whole situation. I so totally don't even think about it anymore. Like ever.)

4 jalapeños

1 cup cheap white vinegar

Slice the jalapeños into 1/8-inch disks, on a mandoline if you have one. Otherwise do it carefully by hand.

Put them in a small container and pour in the vinegar.

Seal the container and put it in the refrigerator until you are ready to party or have the urge to throw spicy vinegar in someone's eyes. This will keep for the rest of time.

Raisin & Scallion Relish

Makes about 2 cups

This little relish doodah is great for adding a sweet and oniony bite to any sandwich. Also, if you put this and a little mustard on a hot dog, you might

start screaming. In terror. Because it'll scare you, how much you like eating it. I like yellow raisins, but I'm not sure what exactly I have against red grapes and the raisins that come from them. I'm also not that into red potatoes. I just googled "why don't I like red grapes?" and all that came up was a bunch of stuff about red wine and dogs, and I'm not super into either of those things, so that may explain it. Sorry, William Wegman!!

1 cup golden raisins, roughly chopped

1 cup sliced scallions*

1 tablespoon olive oil

1 tablespoon vinegar

½ teaspoon kosher salt

* Cookbook editors always want to know if it's the green part, the white part, or the whole scallion. Who the fuck is writing a recipe wherein you can't use the whole scallion? `[Why must you mock our culture? —Ed.]`

Combine the raisins, scallions, olive oil, vinegar, and salt in a medium mixing bowl and stir until well combined. Let sit for 20 minutes before using. Store unused portion in the refrigerator for up to a week.

Spaghetti Squash Salad

Makes about 3 cups

Everybody knows that spaghetti squash is really pretty when you cook it and then shred it into spaghetti-like strands. But did you know that it's also delicious, good for you, and also delicious? Aren't you so glad you bought a used copy of this book so you can learn so much smart from me?

1 medium spaghetti squash, about 3 pounds

1 tablespoon olive oil

3 teaspoons kosher salt, or to taste

3 tablespoons cider vinegar

1 tablespoon sour cream

Preheat the oven to 375°F.

Split the squash lengthwise and scrape out the seeds. Also, if you bought this spaghetti squash at the grocery store, look and see if there is a sticker on the outside of the spaghetti squash. If there is, remove it and keep it in a small plastic container with a tight-fitting lid in the refrigerator. It is the only thing that can stop the alien invasion.

Cut the squash halves crosswise into 2-inch-wide half-moons. In a mixing bowl, toss the squash pieces with the olive oil and 1 teaspoon of salt.

Arrange the squash, skin side down, on a baking sheet and place it in the oven. Cook until the squash is lightly caramelized and fork tender, 30 to 45 minutes, depending on the squash. You want to make sure that it's cooked enough to shred and not be too crunchy, but not so cooked that it's just a pile of mush.

When the squash is cool enough to work with, shred it into a mixing bowl, discarding the skins, and then add the vinegar, sour cream, and remaining salt. Mix everything together thoroughly and chill the salad until ready to serve. This will be good for three to four days.

Haricots Verts Salad

Makes enough for 6 to 8 large sandwiches or a lovely side dish for 4 people

You could make this with regular green beans instead of haricots verts, but you could also go out and get a slice of pizza instead of making this salad. Haricots verts are prettier and smaller, and so I like them better for the salad. That said, if you want to make this salad ahead of time and keep it for a while, then you should use yellow wax beans because the vinaigrette will make haricots verts and green beans turn brown. We haven't even started and this is already getting complicated. Maybe we should just go get that slice of pizza.

1 large or 2 small shallots, sliced thin

3 tablespoons white vinegar

2 tablespoons kosher salt, plus more to taste

3 cups haricots verts, stems removed

1 tablespoon olive oil

In a mixing bowl, combine the shallots and vinegar and let them sit.

Put 2 quarts of water and the salt in a pot and bring to a boil. Add the haricots verts to the pot and boil on high until the beans are bright green and a little crunchy, about 3 minutes. Strain the beans out of the water and transfer to a bowl of ice water to cool.

Remove the beans from the ice bath and combine them in a mixing bowl with the shallots, vinegar, oil, and salt to taste. The vinaigrette that these beans are now sitting in is super intense, so it's okay if you end up leaving some of it in the bowl.

Fried Garlic

Makes about ¼ cup fried garlic and 1 pint garlic oil

If you've never sprinkled fried garlic on ramen noodles or a sandwich, I won't make any judgments about your life and the decisions you make. But you really should try it because it is intense and amazing and I like it as a flavoring component better than bacon.

1 pint vegetable oil

1 head of garlic, each clove sliced paper thin on a mandoline*

* You can do this with a knife instead of a mandoline, but go slow and try to make your slices as even as possible or when you fry them the thin ones will burn before the thick ones get crispy.

Set a fine-mesh sieve over a large metal bowl on a heatproof surface. Line a plate with paper towels.

Add the oil and sliced garlic to a small saucepan.

Set the heat to high and, stirring constantly, cook until the garlic is light brown on the outside and a tiny bit white in the middle. Basically, the garlic should be a shade or two away from the full golden brown you think it should look, because it is going to carry over more than you would expect it to.

Pour the contents of the pot into the sieve and then transfer the drained garlic to the paper towels to cool and drain some more. Let the garlic sit out on the paper towels until cooled completely and then put it in a small, airtight container and put it on food sometimes. Cool down the oil and save it in the fridge for marinating meats or vinaigrettes or making other food delicious or getting your skin to shine bright like a diamond (and smell like garlic).

Shredded Cabbage Salad

Makes about 4 cups, enough for 8 sandwiches or a side dish for 4

This salad is super simple. When I worked at the French Culinary Institute, the dishwashers would make a really simple cabbage salad, and I wanted to eat it all of the time. I think they used vinegar, but for this we'll use lemon juice because I really like cabbage and lemon together. But feel free to make it with vinegar!

½ smallish head of green cabbage, cored and shredded

1 teaspoon kosher salt

1 tablespoon olive oil

2 tablespoons lemon juice

In a large mixing bowl, combine the cabbage, salt, olive oil, and lemon juice. Mix thoroughly. Let stand, refrigerated, for at least 15 minutes and up to a few days.

Avocado Blue Cheese

Makes about ¾ cup

Avocado blue cheese is exactly what it sounds like. Really stinky avocado. And it is super delicious. And spreadable. And you can use an overripe avocado for this and nobody will notice.

1 avocado, pitted and scooped out from the skin

2 tablespoons blue cheese crumbles

1 tablespoon lime juice

In a food processor, combine the avocado, blue cheese, and lime juice. Process until smooth. This is a small amount, so you may want to double it or mix it by hand with a fork if it's not enough food for your food processor to deal with.

Jicama Salad

Makes 1 to 2 cups of salad, depending on the size of your jicama

Jicama is not the most flavorful thing you will ever eat. It is a tuber from South America that is a little sweet, but the thing that makes it rad is its texture—it's light and crunchy, almost like an Asian pear, and it's super righteous on a sandwich because it's not too sweet, so you can use it with other sweet things without worrying about throwing off the balance. Party?

1 medium jicama

1 tablespoon lemon juice

1 tablespoon olive oil

Kosher salt to taste

Listen, I never claimed this was going to be complicated.

Peel the jicama. I would grate it on the large holes of a box grater. If you don't have one of those, you could julienne it, shave it all up with a peeler, or take tiny bites of it and drop them from your mouth into a bowl, like a mother bird feeding her baby birds.

Toss the jicama with the lemon juice and olive oil, and season with salt and keep tasting until it's perfect.

Pickled Bean Sprouts

Makes a lot of pickled bean sprouts

Mung bean sprouts are my favorite bean sprouts. They're so crunchy and awesome. I like them just fine raw, but when they're sautéed, pickled, or blanched, they get a truly amazing texture that is like nothing else. A big bowl of garlicky sautéed mung bean sprouts is just as good, if not better, than any sautéed spinach that I've ever met. I think I first had them pickled at Momofuku Ssäm Bar with some kind of raw fish situation. It had never occurred to me to pickle them, but it's been a favorite ever since.

1 tablespoon sugar

1 tablespoon kosher salt

2 cups white vinegar

1 pound mung bean sprouts*

* You could cut this recipe in half, but I can't buy less than a pound at the Korean market by my house

In a medium mixing bowl, combine the sugar, salt, and vinegar and whisk until totally dissolved. Add 4 cups water and the bean sprouts and transfer to a plastic container with a lid. Store in the refrigerator for up to a month.

Coleslaw

Makes 4 to 5 cups

I like to use red cabbage for my coleslaw just because it is pretty. But green cabbage will work well too.

½ smallish head of red cabbage, cored and shredded

½ carrot, grated

½ red onion, sliced thin

1 tablespoon Fried Garlic (PAGE 180)

4 dill sprigs, chopped all the way to the last inch or so of stem

½ cup Mayo (PAGE 160)

½ cup white vinegar

1 tablespoon sugar

Kosher salt to taste

In a large mixing bowl, combine the cabbage, carrot, onion, fried garlic, dill, mayo, vinegar, and sugar, and mix. Season generously with salt to taste. Stir everything together until thoroughly mixed. Transfer to a plastic container with a lid and store in the refrigerator for at least an hour and up to three or four days.

Basic Potato Chips

Makes a whole lot of potato chips, but how long does a whole lot of potato chips last, really?

Potato chips are easy to make if you just don't mind dealing with some oil when you're done. You can do this. Or you can buy potato chips, but these will be better, I promise! Also, your kitchen will smell like potato chips for another day after you make them!

6 medium Idaho potatoes, about ½ pound each

2 quarts canola oil

Kosher salt to taste

Fill a large, deep container with 10 inches of water. Slice the potatoes into rounds on a mandoline one slice at a time, adjusting the thickness on the mandoline until you find the perfect thickness for your potatoes, which is exactly four hairs thicker than you think it is. Once you find your sweet spot, discard your trial slices and slice the rest of the potatoes into the water. You need all of your slices to be exactly the same, so do not adjust your mandoline halfway through, and be conscious to maintain even pressure with each slice. I don't mean to stress you out, but I cannot emphasize enough the importance of doing this step perfectly; if your slices are uneven, you'll end up with a bowl of dark, overcooked chips mixed with undercooked, less-than-crispy chips. You can do this, but focus and remember your training. Also, be careful not to cut yourself on the mandoline. Maybe use that guard thingie that came with it, or wear an oven mitt, as attractive as that makes you feel.

Let the potatoes sit undisturbed, submerged in the water, for 20 minutes. The water should look clear now, as all of the excess starch from the potatoes has sunk to the bottom.

Place the oil in a pot that seems too tall for this project. When the potatoes go in, they will cause the oil to bubble up, and you don't want it to bubble over. One of those thermometers that clips onto the side of the pot would be helpful right now. Heat the oil over medium-high heat, and shoot for around 350°F.

Line a baking sheet with paper towels.

Pull a handful of potatoes out of the water, give them a few shakes to get rid of excess water, and carefully add them to the oil to fry them. If you put in too many, they won't be as pretty. A small handful should be good unless you have ridiculously huge hands, in which case you should just do half a handful. If you are a meticulous person, you can toss the slices in one at a time, like you're dealing cards to a very dangerous poker player, and that way they will be less likely to stick together.

Don't stir the potatoes until they start to look a little wrinkly. The immense amount of bubbles will push them apart. Some of them may stick together a little, but if you go crazy stirring them right when you put them in, they will get all bunched up. Once they get a little firm and shriveled looking, you should stir them with a slotted spoon until there is no part of a potato that is still white (even if it's just barely got any color) and the bubbling subsides almost totally. The bubbles mean that there is still moisture in your potatoes, and for crispy chips you want as little moisture as possible. The idea is to get them as dry as possible without burning them. It may take a little practice finding the exact right thickness to achieve this, as the thicker ones will take longer and be more likely to get too dark before they get crispy, but once you find that perfect size, you will be a champion.

When you take each batch out, drain them on the paper towels and season them with salt immediately.

BBQ Potato Chip Spice Mix

Makes enough spice mix for all of the potato chips you're likely to ever fry

Look, nobody will get mad if you tap out and go buy some potato chips. This book isn't quite what you thought it would be, and that's not your fault. You just want to get drunk and make sandwiches, and I can't say I blame you. Some crazy spirit is making me write this, or I would stop now. So that blame is entirely on me, not you! Just go get some Kettle Brand Potato Chips. They make some killer baked ones that I know you're going to love.

Are you still reading? Cool. I'm sorry about that last bit; I just wanted to ditch the people who aren't really committed to this. Because I feel that you and I really understand each other, while those other parasites were just sucking the life out of us with their constant whining. Nobody said they had to make potato chips in the first place! But nobody ever told you that you needed to be awesome, and you just do it, each and every goddamn day, because it's more important to be awesome than happy. That is truth.

¼ cup sugar

½ cup salt

2 teaspoons smoked Spanish paprika

½ teaspoon onion powder

½ teaspoon garlic powder

½ teaspoon ground cumin

½ teaspoon ground coriander

½ teaspoon ancho chile powder

½ teaspoon chipotle chile powder

Combine all of the ingredients in a bowl and mix well. Technically speaking, you could toast this mixture a little, but it's not entirely necessary because when the spice mix hits those blazing hot sliced potatoes with their thin layer of oil, they'll instantly toast a little and the flavors will come out.

Follow the recipe for Basic Potato Chips (page 182) and at the end, instead of seasoning them with salt, season them with a healthy amount of this spice mix.

I want to be very clear that this spice mix will make more than you need for a single batch of Basic Potato Chips, so don't go crazy thinking you have to use it all up. Use what you need and seal the rest in an airtight container or an enemy's shoes and use it when you need it—unless you chose the enemy's shoes route, in which case you should pretend you don't know anything about it. And definitely don't ask the enemy for the spice mix back or they will know that you put it in their shoes.

Sandwich Construction: Theory & a Chart

It's important to achieve balance in sandwiches, because who really knows how to achieve it in life? Life is messy, difficult, occasionally great but mostly upsetting and out of your control. But you can always make a good sandwich, and a good sandwich will make you happy!

So after dozens of sandwich recipes and a whole bunch of recipes for ingredients, you should feel free to make your own super-crazy sandwiches out of any of the things in this book or anything you have in your fridge. Make a sandwich out of sandwiches! But there is a secret for success in inventing your own sandwiches . . . or at least a theory.

Sandwiches are governed by the basic rule of delicious food: They should have contrast and harmony. What that means is that each component of a sandwich should make the others more awesome, usually by making up for what the other stuff lacks. For a truly awesome sandwich, we want to put these things between bread:

Something Salty and Substantial
Something Fatty
Something Acidic
Something Sweet
Something Crunchy

Sometimes you can achieve all of these somethings with just a few components. Take, for example, a cheeseburger with ketchup and french fries on it. The burger is salty, substantial, and fatty; the ketchup is acidic and sweet; and the french fries are crunchy.

Let's try another one. First, think about what makes you happiest. The answer is probably fried chicken. If you're thinking, "No, my dog and my friends are what make me happiest!" when was the last time that fried chicken slobbered all over your rug or posted a picture on the Internet of you dancing topless on a bar? You really need to rethink your own happiness. Fried chicken is pretty easy to make a great sandwich from because it's already salty, substantial, fatty, and, if you followed the recipe correctly, crunchy. That only leaves sweet and acidic. You can break out the bread-and-butter pickles, which knock out both the sweet and sour, and you'd also have a pretty classic sandwich. But there are about a thousand things that would add an awesome acidity to this sandwich and about a million things that could add sweetness.

Let's start with the acid. Lactic acid from fermented pickles or vinegar from quick pickles is a great choice. But what else is sour? If you take anything from this book, let it be this question: "What else is X?"—X meaning whatever flavor, texture, smell, or attitude that you are trying to convey. Potato chips are crunchy; what else is crunchy? Peaches are sweet; what else is sweet? Clams are salty; what else is salty? So, pickles are sour, right, but what else is sour? Wine can be sour, sauerkraut is sour, and Atomic Warheads are crazy sour. Rhubarb is sour and fun, and how often do you eat rhubarb? Carrots are sweet, and if you simmer carrots with a little salt, some chopped-up rhubarb, and some orange juice until they are glazed and put them in your fried chicken sandwich, I'll bet you will be pleased. I've never made that; I'm just guessing. But I'm probably right.

Now let's look at broccoli, because I really like broccoli. Roast some broccoli (see page 56) and toss it with some Shallot-Ginger Vinaigrette (page 166). It's substantial, salty, and acidic. We still need something fatty, something sweet, and something crunchy. What is fatty? Well, mayonnaise is mostly fat, but you are looking for adventure. Salmon is fatty. A roasted broccoli sandwich with smoked salmon would be pretty incredible. But duck is ridiculously fatty, and it has the potential for crispy too. Let's say you have a couple of duck legs and roast them in a 250°F oven for a couple of hours, skin side up. When you pick that meat and skin off of the bone you will have a very happy sandwich addition. And everybody knows that oranges are sweet and go great with duck, so let's not let everybody down. Why not spread a little bit of orange marmalade on that sandwich? After all, your orange beef from Great Wall No. 1 Chinese Restaurant always comes with steamed broccoli!

So, when making sandwiches, I always think about balancing these characteristics and components to achieve optimum rock and roll. From there, the trick is just figuring out how much to use of which ingredient so nothing overpowers the rest, which is easy: Start with a little of something, taste, and add a little more until it's awesome. Here's a chart to get you thinking:

Substantial	*Fatty*	*Acidic*	*Sweet*	*Crunchy*
cauliflower	bacon	citrus	beets	bacon
cold cuts	butter	fermented pickles	carrots	raw carrots
leftover turkey	cheese	green apple	fruit	cereal
eggplant	duck fat	raspberries	hoisin sauce	crackers
fried chicken	mayo	sour cream	honey	egg rolls
depression	olive oil	stress	jelly/jam	fried chicken skin
pulled pork	scrambled eggs	verjus	maple syrup	fried shallots
roast beef	pâté or smoked fish pâté	vinaigrette	marshmallows	potato chips
smoked trout	sour cream	vinegar	pineapple	nuts
zucchini	creamy dressing	wine	sweet potatoes	hippies

And that's just off the top of my head. You should look around your kitchen and fill in your own chart. A leftover turkey sandwich with mayo, pineapple, hoisin sauce, and fried shallots sounds pretty perfect right now, though. But maybe that's me.

ACKNOWLEDGMENTS

It feels a little strange to thank people for their help with this book, considering that they may, in the end, be embarrassed by it or have to distance themselves from it. But I'm going to do it anyway, and they may all sue me, and I'll just have to live with that.

To my boobaloo Katherine Pangaro, you work harder than anyone I've ever met, and it blows my mind every day. I do not know what I would do without you. And luckily you are stuck with me so I won't ever have to find out. And I know that I owe you a vacation.

To my partner and best buddy Matthew Maddy, you somehow always get everything right and you never get enough credit for it and this is not enough but I'm trying. That said, you are smarter, funnier, taller, and better looking than me, so I don't feel super bad.

To my partner and nonbiological brother Ian Sugarman, your belief in my abilities is humbling, and while I am constantly sure that I will fail, you are constantly pushing me farther, and that has been invaluable. And you kind of made *Star Wars*, so there's also that.

To all of the management and staff at No. 7, No. 7 Sub, and No. 7 North, thank you for helping me make so many people happy every day. None of this would exist without you guys, and I appreciate each and every one of you.

To my mother, Betty Kord, you made something different for dinner every night for the first eighteen years of my life, and it was always delicious. But you worry about me too much, and this book probably won't help matters! Everything will be okay, I promise! I will call you tomorrow.

To my father, Victor Kord, you are the most knowledgeable person I have ever met and one of the greatest artists the world will ever know. I hope that someday I can be half the man that you are. And I know that I owe you lunch.

To my sister, brother-in-law, and nephews: Emily, Luca, Matteo, and James, you guys are the greatest and you know it. I'm sorry that I'm not always the best brother/in-law/uncle.

To the man that made me the coolest shoes of all time, Doug Palladini, I am constantly impressed that a dude with so much power and responsibility can also be so incredibly warm and caring and lets me be a part of one of the coolest companies in the world. And of course, I wouldn't even know you were it not for Ryan DeWitt. I miss him like crazy and wish he could have seen this book finished.

To my editor, Francis Lam, I didn't really love working with you, but I'm sure yule "edit" this to say something super nice. Just don't use any of those totally effected British terms your so fond of. They make you sound needie. Ask Christine. She'll tell you what I'm talking about.

To the incredible team that worked on this book with me, Maggie Ruggiero, Noah Fecks, Michael Nagin, and Ian Dingman, there would obviously be no book without you guys, and it was a genuine pleasure and an honor to have your collective talent harnessed to make something so stupid, and I feel like you all just did it because you like me and that means the world.

To my nonbiological uncle William Wegman, I still can't believe you agreed to do this, and I'm so sorry if you regret it! You are probably the only reason anybody will buy this book, and I am completely okay with that.

To the countless others, of whom there are too many to name (but I'll name a few), who have helped along the way: Ryan Reynolds, Chris Fischer, Meg Moorhouse, Amanda Clarke, Gabriel Llanos, Eric Sell, Jeff Maslanka, Jared Glenn, Kathryn Weatherup, Johnathan Wu, E-Boogie, Sebastian Okrasa, Anthony Trotman, and James Caputo. Thank you all so much.

And lastly, to my agent, Jonah Straus, I still can't believe you convinced somebody to buy this crazy book. Nice fucking work, dude.

DKNY

Index

Published in the United States
by Clarkson Potter/Publishers, an
imprint of the Crown Publishing
Group, a division of Penguin
Random House LLC, New York.
www.crownpublishing.com
www.clarksonpotter.com

CLARKSON POTTER is a
trademark and POTTER with
colophon is a registered trademark of
Penguin Random House LLC.

Library of Congress
Cataloging-in-Publication Data
Kord, Tyler, author.
A super upsetting cookbook about
sandwiches / Tyler Kord ;
photographs by Noah Fecks ;
artwork by William Wegman.
pages cm
Includes index.
1. Sandwiches. I. Fecks, Noah,
photographer. II. Title.
TX818.K67 2016
641.84—dc23 2015028505

ISBN 978-0-804-18641-4
eISBN 978-0-804-18642-1

Printed in China

Book design by Ian Dingman
Cover design by Ian Dingman
Cover photography by Noah Fecks
Food styling by Maggie Ruggiero

5 7 9 10 8 6

First Edition

TURKEY MEATLOAF
VEGGIE BURGER
ASPARAGUS
ROAST BEEF
CARROT PUREE
VELVEETA
SHREDDED CABBAGE SALAD
MARINARA SAUCE
CHI
HOW SOON IS NOW
SHALLOT-GINGER VINAIGRETTE
CUCUMBER MUCHIM
CILANTRO
FETA CHEESE
(HIS NAME IS) ROBERT PAULSON
LETTUCE
BACON MAYO
GENTLE THOUGH
TOMATO
PICKLED BEAN SPROUTS
HOT ROAST BEEF
JALAP
JUS
GENERAL TSO'S FRIED FISH
BBQ CH
MOZZARELLA
CHORIZO
RO
COLE SLAW
DIRTY TARTAR SAUCE
ROASTED ONIONS
ALTERED BEEF
FAMOUS RAP BATTLES OF HISTORY
MUENST
SOPPRESSATA
ROASTED CHICKEN
BLACK BEAN HUMMUS
PORK & SHRIMP SAUSAGE
THAI BASIL
ROASTED ONIONS
TOMATO
LETTUCE
FRITOS
MICHELADA MAYO
CHICKEN-FRIED MUSHROOM
TOMATO
THE FRITO KID
CILANTRO
TEXAS-WISCONSIN BORDER
PEACH MUCH
ROASTED BROCCOLI
PINE NUTS
GRILLED SQUID & ZUCCHINI
RED ONIONS
LIME
THE SUZAN SUGARBAK
RICOTTA SALATA
FORT GREENE GODDESS DRESSING
ASPARAGUS
GREEN OLIVES
LYCHEE MUCHIM
ROASTED TOM
TYLER KORD ON CUYLER GORE
FRIED GARLIC
BROCCOLI CLASSIC
CHEDDAR
COLD MEATLOAF
POACHED ARCTIC CHAR
AVOCADO RICOTTA
TOMATO MUCHIM
HARICOTS VERTS SA
CUCUMBER MUCHIM
BACON MAYO
HOT PATOOTIE
SPAGHETTI SQUASH SALAD
FRIE
FRIED SHALLOTS
THE SHADIEST ONE
BIBB LETTUCE
BL
ROASTED ONIONS
THE B OF SH
VEGGIE BURGER
GENERAL TSO'S TOFU
CHEESE
PATTY MELT!
PICKLED GINGER
ZUCCHINI PARM
FRIED ZUCCHINI
PICKLED JALAPEÑOS
ROAS
MAYO
FRIED
FONTINA
ONION PUREE
BBQ POTATO CHIPS
SHISO
FRESH MOZ